Greek Mythology

Mythical Beasts & the Beliefs of Ancient Greece

(A Concise Guide to the Ancient Gods and Beliefs of Egyptian Mythology)

Joseph Joyner

Published By **Darby Connor**

Joseph Joyner

All Rights Reserved

Greek Mythology: Mythical Beasts & the Beliefs of Ancient Greece (A Concise Guide to the Ancient Gods and Beliefs of Egyptian Mythology)

ISBN 978-1-7772550-8-4

No part of this guidebook shall be reproduced in any form without permission in writing from the publisher except in the case of brief quotations embodied in critical articles or reviews.

Legal & Disclaimer

The information contained in this book is not designed to replace or take the place of any form of medicine or professional medical advice. The information in this book has been provided for educational & entertainment purposes only.

The information contained in this book has been compiled from sources deemed reliable, and it is accurate to the best of the Author's knowledge; however, the Author cannot guarantee its accuracy and validity and cannot be held liable for any errors or omissions. Changes are periodically made to this book. You must consult your doctor or get professional medical advice before using any of the suggested remedies, techniques, or information in this book.

Upon using the information contained in this book, you agree to hold harmless the Author from and against any damages, costs, and expenses, including any legal fees potentially resulting from the application of any of the information provided by this guide. This disclaimer applies to any damages or injury caused by the use and application, whether directly or indirectly, of any advice or information presented, whether for breach of contract, tort, negligence, personal injury, criminal intent, or under any other cause of action.

You agree to accept all risks of using the information presented inside this book. You need to consult a professional medical practitioner in order to ensure you are both able and healthy enough to participate in this program.

Table Of Contents

Chapter 1: Zeus King of the Gods 1

Chapter 2: Hera Queen of the Gods 9

Chapter 3: Poseidon God of the Sea 19

Chapter 4: Demeter Goddess of Agriculture 31

Chapter 5: Athena Goddess of Wisdom and Warfare 42

Chapter 6: God of War 70

Chapter 7: Aphrodite Goddess of Love and Beauty 80

Chapter 8: Hephaestus God of Blacksmiths and Fire 93

Chapter 9: Hermes Messenger of the Gods 105

Chapter 10: Hades God of the Underworld 117

Chapter 11: The Origins of Greek Mythology 138

Chapter 12: Heroes and Heroines 149

Chapter 13: Greek Myths in Literature. 157

Chapter 14: Lesser Deities and Creatures 162

Chapter 15: The Trojan War a Tale of Heroes and Destiny 167

Chapter 16: Love and Desire 174

Chapter 17: The Quests and Adventures 180

Chapter 1: Zeus King of the Gods

Zeus is one of the maximum splendid figures in Greek mythology and occupies a crucial area inside the Greek pantheon due to the fact the king of the godsHere's an exploration of Zeus's location inside the pantheon, which incorporates his parentage and siblings:

Parentage:

Zeus's parentage is a crucial component of his feature in Greek mythologyHe changed into the son of Cronus (moreover known as Kronos) and RheaCronus changed into one of the Titans, a race of effective deities who ruled in advance than the Olympian godsHowever, Cronus became fearful of a prophecy that one in every of his kids ought to overthrow him, so he devoured his offspring as rapid as they have been bornTo save Zeus from this destiny, Rhea tricked Cronus via giving him a stone wrapped in a little one's blanket, at the equal time as she hid Zeus away.

Siblings:

Zeus had severa siblings, most of whom had been swallowed with the aid of way of Cronus earlier than they will advantage adulthoodThese siblings embody:

Hestia: The firstborn of Cronus and Rhea, Hestia modified into the goddess of the fireplace and homeShe is often depicted as a slight and nurturing figure.

Hera: Hera modified into Zeus's sister and, later, his spouseShe became the goddess of marriage and childbirth and performed a extensive position in Greek mythology because the queen of the gods.

Demeter: Demeter come to be the goddess of agriculture and the harvestHer daughter Persephone become abducted through Hades, most important to the arrival of the seasons.

Hades: Hades, the god of the underworld, modified into Zeus's brotherHe ruled over the realm of the useless and become now not typically counted most of the twelve Olympian gods, as he not often resided on Mount Olympus.

Poseidon: Poseidon, a few one of a kind brother of Zeus, turn out to be the god of the sea, storms, and earthquakesHe wielded a trident and have become a powerful and unpredictable deity.

Hestia (over again): After Zeus's transport, Rhea gave Cronus a 2nd stone wrapped in a infant's blanket, and this time, Hestia have become saved.

Chiron (in some variations): Chiron have grow to be a clever centaur who turn out to be frequently taken into consideration a sibling or 1/2 of-sibling of ZeusHe come to be seemed for his attention and abilities in treatment and the humanities.

Zeus's Role in the Pantheon:

Zeus emerged because the leader of the Olympian gods after a battle called the Titanomachy, during which the Olympians, led thru Zeus, overthrew the Titans and mounted their reign on Mount OlympusAs the king of the gods, Zeus wielded massive energy and authorityHe have grow to be the god of the sky, thunder, and lightning, frequently depicted with a thunderbolt in his handZeus's function prolonged to different factors of life, collectively with justice, law, and order.

Zeus have end up stated for his unpredictable nature and his numerous affairs and marriages, which resulted inside the beginning of many demigods and heroes in Greek mythologyHe come to be moreover responsible for upholding the divine order and punishing those who defied it.

In precis, Zeus changed right into a critical discern in the Greek pantheon, every in phrases of his parentage and his function because the king of the godsHis siblings, who have been each swallowed with the resource of Cronus or survived in thriller, accomplished large roles in Greek mythology as nicely, together forming the pantheon of gods and goddesses worshipped by means of the historic Greeks.

Personality Traits:

Authoritative: Zeus is the exceptional ruler of the Olympian gods, and he embodies authority and electricityHe is regularly depicted as a commanding determine who expects obedience from each gods and mortals.

Just and Fair: Zeus is frequently visible as a god of justice and orderHe serves as a divine pick, settling disputes a number of the gods and peopleHis options are usually visible as honest, notwithstanding the fact that his judgments may be inspired with the aid of the usage of personal biases at instances.

Protective: Zeus is protecting of his circle of relatives and people he favorsHe can be wrathful and vengeful even as someone threatens his loved ones or disturbing situations his authority.

Lover of Beauty: Zeus has a popularity for his amorous pastimesHe had numerous affairs and fathered many demigods and heroesThis element of his personality presentations his appreciation for splendor and the human revel in.

Wise and Strategic: As the ruler of the gods, Zeus presentations records and strategic thinkingHe often plans his moves cautiously, mainly in managing demanding situations to his rule or the divine order.

Motivations:

Maintaining Order: One of Zeus's number one motivations is to uphold the cosmic order (referred to as "cosmic justice" or "divine order")He seeks to ensure that the sector and the gods function harmoniously and justly.

Protecting His Dominion: Zeus is fiercely shielding of his characteristic as king of the gods and could visit terrific lengths to preserve his authority and protect his circle of relatives.

Enjoyment of Life: Zeus is understood for his indulgence inside the pleasures of existence, together with food, drink, and the organization of different gods and mortalsHis amorous escapades are frequently driven through using the usage of his preference for pleasure and beauty.

Symbols:

Thunderbolt: The most iconic image related to Zeus is the thunderboltHe is regularly depicted wielding a thunderbolt, representing his manipulate over the skies, thunder, and lightning.

Eagle: The eagle is considered the sacred hen of ZeusIt is visible as a image of his electricity and authority and is from time to time depicted as his messenger.

Scepter: Zeus is regularly portrayed maintaining a scepter, a photo of his rule and authority as king of the gods.

Olympian Throne: Zeus's throne on Mount Olympus is a image of his kingship and primary characteristic inside the pantheon.

Aegis: Zeus sometimes wore the aegis, a protecting cloak or shield related to him, frequently bearing the top of the Gorgon MedusaIt served as a symbol of his divine protection and authority.

Chapter 2: Hera Queen of the Gods

Hera is a remarkable decides in Greek mythology and a member of the Olympian pantheon, the institution of deities who ruled Mount Olympus, the very best pinnacle in GreeceHer lineage in the pantheon is a key aspect of her identity and function an effect on in Greek mythology.

Hera changed into the daughter of Cronus and Rhea, two of the Titans who ruled in advance than the Olympian gods got here to powerCronus, worried that in reality taken into consideration considered one of his kids might also overthrow him as he had overthrown his very personal father, Uranus, swallowed each of his youngsters rapidly after their transportHowever, Rhea managed to save Zeus, her youngest infant, by secretly giving Cronus a stone wrapped in swaddling clothes as a substitute.

Zeus ultimately grew up and, with the assist of his mom and different allies, led a upward thrust up closer to Cronus and the TitansIn the Titanomachy, the first-rate struggle among the Titans and the Olympians, Zeus emerged a hit, and the Olympian gods took their region because the rulers of the cosmos.

As one of the children of Cronus and Rhea, Hera have become one of the Olympian deities, and he or she married her brother Zeus, becoming the queen of the godsHer marriage to Zeus solidified her reputation as one of the chief goddesses within the Greek pantheon, and he or she or he or he performed a huge position in numerous myths and stories throughout Greek mythology.

Personality and Attributes:

Matronly and Protective: Hera is often depicted as a maternal decide in Greek mythology, emphasizing her feature because the protector of marriage and the familyShe is answerable for overseeing the properly-being and concord of married couples and their offspring.

Jealous and Vengeful: One of Hera's maximum well-known trends is her jealousy, specially concerning her husband Zeus's many affairs with mortal women and goddessesHer jealousy frequently leads her to trying to find revenge toward Zeus's fans and their illegitimate kids.

Powerful and Regal: As the queen of the gods and one of the Olympians, Hera possesses massive electricity and authorityShe is frequently portrayed as regal and dignified, representing the divine order and the organization of marriage.

Fidelity and Chastity: Despite her jealousy and vengeful nature, Hera herself is associated with fidelity and chastity in marriageShe expects the identical from mortal ladies and considers infidelity a grave offense.

Protector of Women: Hera is also seen as a protector of women, specifically for the duration of childbirthShe may be invoked for help in topics related to women's fitness and properly-being.

Motivations:

Protecting Her Domain: Hera's number one motivation is to protect her place, which includes marriage, circle of relatives, and the sanctity of the marital bondShe is deeply committed to preserving order and stability within those regions.

Jealousy and Revenge: Hera's jealousy stems from her desire to keep her function due to the fact the queen of the gods and her resentment of Zeus's infidelityHer motivations for looking for revenge toward Zeus's fans and illegitimate youngsters are pushed thru her anger and feel of betrayal.

Defending Her Honor: Hera often sees Zeus's infidelity as an affront to her honor and dignityHer moves, driven via her experience of pride and righteousness, intention to defend her recognition and assert her authority.

Hera's divine powers

Blessing Marriages:

Hera changed into believed to preside over weddings and marriagesCouples would possibly invoke her to are searching for for her blessings for a harmonious and fruitful union.

Her presence changed into regularly invoked sooner or later of wedding ceremony ceremonies to make certain the sanctity of the marital bond and to shield the newlyweds from damage.

Fertility and Childbirth:

Hera had a proper away have an impact on on fertility and childbirthShe changed into considered a goddess who may additionally want to furnish or withhold the functionality to conceive and endure youngsters.

Women prayed to Hera for help in conceiving youngsters and for a stable and wholesome childbirth revel inThey furnished prayers and sacrifices to advantage her preference.

Protecting Mothers and Children:

Hera become appeared as a father or mother of expectant moms and their offspringShe grow to be often invoked to shield women during pregnancy and childbirth.

Her protecting characteristic prolonged to each mortal and divine pregnanciesIn mythology, she done a function inside the births of numerous important figures, together with Hercules (Heracles), whom she tried to thwart because of his being a product of Zeus's infidelity.

Enforcing Marital Fidelity:

Hera modified into particularly worried with upholding the sanctity of marriage and enforcing fidelity inside the marital relationship.

She took her function due to the fact the protector of marriage very critically and punished people who violated the marriage vows, often centered on Zeus's numerous lovers and their illegitimate kids.

Divine Authority:

As the queen of the gods, Hera's divine authority extended to subjects of governance in the Olympian pantheonShe held wonderful effect in divine selection-making and feature grow to be identified for her assertiveness in council conferences some of the gods.

Moral and Ethical Guidance:

Hera's have an effect on over marriage and family life moreover extended to guiding mortals in topics of ethics and moralityShe served as a photograph of marital constancy and have become often invoked as a ethical instance.

Symbolic Representations:

In innovative representations, Hera emerge as regularly depicted carrying a crown or diadem, emphasizing her regal reputationShe additionally carried a scepter as a image of her authority.

The pomegranate, a picture of fertility and abundance, modified into related to Hera, highlighting her connection to childbirth and the nurturing additives of her place.

Hera's divine powers and feature an impact on over marriage and childbirth showcased her function as a protector of the circle of relatives unit and a symbol of marital determinationWhile her man or woman have become often portrayed with complexities, together collectively along with her jealousy and vengeful nature, her importance in Greek mythology within the ones domains cannot be deniedHer function have turn out to be vital in the cultural and non secular framework of ancient Greece, emphasizing the significance of marriage and the circle of relatives inside society.

Unfolding Hera's Role in Various Myths and Her Interactions with Other Gods

Hera plays a super feature in numerous myths and interactions with specific gods in Greek mythologyHere are some exceptional myths and instances showcasing her person and relationships:

The Marriage of Hera and Zeus:

One of the maximum terrific myths concerning Hera is her marriage to Zeus, her brotherTheir union marked them because the king and queen of the Olympian godsDespite Zeus's many infidelities, Hera remained his partner and maintained her function as queen.

The Birth of Hephaestus:

In one fantasy, Hera gave shipping to Hephaestus (or Vulcan), the god of blacksmiths and craftsmen, with out the involvement of ZeusSome variations of the myth propose that Hephaestus was conceived parthenogenetically or that Hera bore him in reaction to Zeus's movementsShe later rejected Hephaestus due to his physical deformities.

Chapter 3: Poseidon God of the Sea

Poseidon holds a large region within the Greek pantheon as one of the twelve Olympian gods, ruling over the seas, waters, and earthquakesHis parentage and siblings are critical factors of his mythology and divine identification:

Parentage:

Poseidon modified into the son of Cronus, the Titan god of time, and Rhea, the Titaness of fertility and motherhoodCronus and Rhea have been a part of the preceding technology of deities referred to as the TitansPoseidon changed into, therefore, a member of the second technology of gods, the Olympians, who overthrew the Titans to count on control of the cosmos.

Siblings:

Zeus: Poseidon's most distinguished sibling emerge as Zeus, the king of the gods and ruler of Mount OlympusAfter the Titans' defeat, Zeus, Poseidon, and Hades drew plenty to determine their domain namesZeus acquired the sky and have become the ruler of the heavens, even as Poseidon claimed dominion over the seas and waters.

Hades: Hades, Poseidon's fantastic sibling, drew the lot for the Underworld, becoming the ruler of the region of the vainTogether, the three brothers customary the middle of the Olympian pantheon and performed key roles in the governance of the universe.

Role and Attributes:

Poseidon's function because the god of the seas and waters made him a important parent in Greek mythology and the lives of sailors, fishermen, and coastal corporationsSome of his attributes and roles embody:

God of the Sea: Poseidon turn out to be chargeable for the great oceans, the turbulent seas, and the creatures that inhabited themSailors and seafarers frequently prayed to him for stable voyages and protection in the course of storms.

Earthshaker: Poseidon changed into additionally known as the "Earthshaker" due to his association with earthquakesHe have grow to be believed to cause earthquakes at the same time as he struck his trident (his divine weapon) on the ground.

Protector of Coastal Cities: Poseidon modified into the client deity of many coastal cities, collectively with Athens, in which he contested with Athena (the goddess of information) for the city's desireHis mark can be seen inside the well-known Temple of Poseidon at Cape Sounion.

Creation of the Horse: In some myths, Poseidon done a role in developing the ponyHe struck the floor along alongside along with his trident, and from the earth sprang forth horses, symbolizing his strength over the land further to the sea.

Personification of the Sea's Dual Nature: Poseidon's temperament have end up regularly as unpredictable as the ocean itselfHe is probably benevolent and calm the waters, or he may be vengeful and stir up violent storms and tempests.

Personality Traits:

Temperamental: Poseidon is concept for his frequently unpredictable and tempestuous nature, mirroring the tumultuous and ever-converting seaHis moods can shift from calm and serene to furious and negative in a direct.

Proud and Assertive: As one of the Olympian gods, Poseidon consists of a strong enjoy of pleasure and authorityHe expects appreciate and reputation for his dominion over the seas and waters, and he may be fiercely defensive of his realm.

Vengeful: Poseidon is infamous for his vengeful dispositions, specially at the same time as he feels slighted or dishonoredHe does now not take demanding situations to his authority lightly and may reply with detrimental acts, which includes inflicting storms, shipwrecks, or earthquakes.

Powerful and Majestic: Poseidon's man or woman is imbued with the majesty and power of the oceanHe is often depicted as a regal parent, carrying a trident, which symbolizes his manipulate over the waters and his capacity to purpose earthquakes.

Protector and Benefactor: While Poseidon can be wrathful, he is likewise visible as a protector and benefactor of sailors, fishermen, and coastal businessesHe is invoked for steady voyages and bountiful catches, showcasing his twin nature as a deity who can both bless and punish.

Motivations:

Assertion of Dominance: Poseidon's number one motivation is to say his dominance over his domains, particularly the seas and watersHe seeks recognition and reverence from mortals and fellow gods alike, striving to maintain his repute as one of the Olympians.

Guardianship: Poseidon is endorsed to guard and watch over the creatures and geographical areas under his manipulate, which include sea creatures, coastal areas, and underwater geographical regionsHis movements can be driven thru a desire to preserve the stability and order of his dominion.

Response to Disrespect: Poseidon's vengeful movements are often inspired with the useful resource of perceived disrespect or defianceHe punishes those who project his authority or display irreverence within the path of him, now and again foremost to unfavourable outcomes.

Symbols:

Trident: Poseidon's maximum iconic picture is his trident, a 3-pronged weapon related to his control over the seaIt represents his authority and strength, and he's often depicted preserving it.

Horses: Horses are symbolically linked to Poseidon, as he turned into believed to have created them via putting the floor collectively with his tridentThey symbolize his connection to both land and sea.

Dolphin: The dolphin is a sacred animal to Poseidon and is frequently depicted along himDolphins are taken into consideration his messengers and are related to secure navigation and the safety of sailors.

Sea Creatures: Poseidon is now and again represented with sea creatures, along facet fish and sea serpents, to emphasize his dominion over the marine international.

Water Imagery: Poseidon is regularly depicted with water imagery, along with seashells, waves, and seascapes, to enhance his affiliation with the ocean and its massive, ever-changing nature.

Powers:

Control Over the Sea:

Poseidon's primary location is the sea, and he has absolute manage over its elementsHe can control the waters, developing calm seas or summoning storms and turbulent wavesHis control extends to all bodies of water, collectively with oceans, seas, lakes, and rivers.

Earthquakes:

Poseidon is often known as the "Earthshaker" due to the truth he wields the strength to motive earthquakesHe can strike the ground along along with his trident, sending shockwaves via the Earth's crust, ensuing in seismic hobby and tremors.

Creation and Manipulation of Storms:

As the god of the sea, Poseidon can create and manage storms of considerable strengthHe can conjure thunderstorms, hurricanes, and tempests, wreaking havoc on the seas and coastal areas.

Summoning Marine Creatures:

Poseidon has the ability to summon and talk with marine creatures, along side dolphins, whales, and sea nymphsThese creatures often function his messengers and helpers, assisting sailors and sporting out his will inside the depths of the sea.

Transformation and Shape-Shifting:

Like many Greek deities, Poseidon possesses the power of shape-movingHe can anticipate diverse paperwork, both human and marine, to have interaction with mortals and unique gods as he pleases.

Blessing and Cursing the Seas:

Poseidon can bestow blessings or curses upon the seas and people who sail upon themSailors would possibly offer prayers and sacrifices to assuage him and gain his want for secure voyages.

Creation of Springs and Fountains:

Poseidon is likewise related to freshwater resourcesHe can create springs, fountains, and freshwater streams, providing a balance amongst his dominion over the ocean and his have an impact on on land.

Powerful Weaponry:

Poseidon wields a trident as his divine weaponThis 3-pronged workforce symbolizes his authority over the waters and may be used every as a device and a weapon to manipulate the sea, create earthquakes, and defend in the direction of threats.

Weather Manipulation:

His manage over the ocean regularly extends to the weatherPoseidon may have an impact on atmospheric situations, at the aspect of winds and cloud formations, to in shape his skills, in addition emphasizing his power over maritime affairs.

Protection and Destruction of Coastal Cities:

Poseidon is the consumer deity of numerous coastal towns and areasHe can defend the ones groups from harm however can also moreover unharness his wrath, causing floods or other disasters within the occasion that they incur his displeasure.

Ability to Challenge and Compete:

Poseidon is thought for his competitiveness and willingness to venture precise gods or beings for dominionThis is visible in myths wherein he contests with Athena for the patronage of Athens or engages in rivalries with specific gods.

key moments from his mythological journeys:

The Battle of the Titans:

Poseidon turn out to be involved in the epic conflict called the Titanomachy, where he and his fellow Olympians waged conflict in competition to the Titans, the older generation of godsIn this war, Poseidon tested his electricity over the seas by manner of developing big waves and storms to beneficial aid the Olympians of their victory.

Creation of Horses:

One of Poseidon's journeys led him to the land, wherein he struck the earth collectively together with his trident, giving upward push to the number one horsesThis act showcased his creative skills and his connection to each land and sea.

Chapter 4: Demeter Goddess of Agriculture

Demeter, a tremendous determines in Greek mythology, holds a great area inside the pantheon because the goddess of agriculture, fertility, and the harvestHer parentage and siblings are critical elements of her divine identity:

Parentage:

Demeter was the daughter of Titans, Cronus and RheaIn Greek mythology, Cronus and Rhea were people of the earlier era of deities known as the TitansDemeter's begin befell inside the path of this pre-Olympian generation.

Siblings:

Zeus: Demeter's maximum notable sibling have become Zeus, her younger brotherZeus emerge as one of the Titans who led the Olympian gods in their rise up inside the path of the TitansHe sooner or later have turn out to be the king of the gods and ruler of Mount Olympus.

Hestia, Hera, Hades, and Poseidon: Demeter had severa special siblings, which incorporates Hestia, Hera, Hades, and PoseidonHestia and Hera have end up critical goddesses in their personal right, with Hestia presiding over the fireside and Hera becoming the queen of the godsHades ruled the Underworld, and Poseidon became the god of the ocean.

Role and Attributes:

Demeter's function inside the Greek pantheon is broadly speakme related to agriculture and the cycle of fertilityHer attributes and roles embody:

Goddess of Agriculture and Fertility: Demeter is fine known as the goddess of agriculture, responsible for the increase of plant life and the fertility of the earthShe was revered via farmers and people who relied on the land for their livelihoods.

Harvest Goddess: Demeter presided over the harvest, and he or she or he changed into specially related to the harvest of grain, particularly wheat and barleyShe ensured the abundance of flowers and the well-being of agricultural organizations.

Maternal and Protective Figure: Demeter have become furthermore a maternal decide, often depicted as a being concerned and protecting motherHer love for her daughter, Persephone, is a great topic in Greek mythology.

Mourning and Grief: Demeter's feelings and movements have been closely tied to the myth of her daughter's abduction thru way of HadesDuring this time, she withdrew her benefits from the earth, resulting in a barren and desolate landscapeThis episode was the idea for the changing seasons in Greek mythology.

Character Traits:

Nurturing and Maternal: Demeter is often portrayed as a nurturing and maternal parent, reflecting her function due to the fact the goddess of agricultureShe cares for the earth like a mom tending to her children, making sure the boom of flora and the well-being of corporations.

Emotional and Protective: Demeter's man or woman is marked with the beneficial resource of sturdy emotions, particularly her love for her daughter, PersephoneHer protecting instincts are evident even as Persephone is kidnapped through Hades, important to

Demeter's deep grief and her moves to normal her daughter's return.

Determined and Tenacious: When faced with adversity, which includes Persephone's abduction, Demeter indicates electricity of thoughts and tenacityShe searches tirelessly for her daughter and takes moves that affect the complete global to explicit her grief and desires.

Vengeful and Capricious: In her grief, Demeter will become vengeful, withholding her advantages from the earth and inflicting famineHer movements, at the same time as comprehensible given the conditions, show her capability for capriciousness and the power of her feelings.

Motivations:

Motherly Love: Demeter's primary motivation is her deep love for her daughter, PersephoneHer grief over Persephone's abduction drives her movements, together with her quest to reunite collectively

collectively along with her daughter and her withholding of agricultural advantages until her daughter's skip again.

Protector of Agriculture: As the goddess of agriculture, Demeter's motivation is to make certain the fertility of the land and the abundance of floraHer advantages are essential for the well-being of humanity, motivating her to care for the earth and its agricultural productiveness.

Seeking Justice: Demeter's quest for justice and retribution in competition to the ones accountable for Persephone's abduction, in particular Zeus and Hades, is a few exceptional key motivationShe wishes that her daughter be decrease lower back to her and seeks to keep those accountable for their actions.

Notable Symbols:

Sheaf of Wheat: The sheaf of wheat is considered definitely certainly one of Demeter's most iconic symbols, representing her function because the goddess of agriculture and the harvestIt symbolizes the abundance of flora and the fertility of the earth

Torch: The torch is a photo of Demeter's look for her daughter, Persephone, after she is kidnapped thru HadesIt moreover symbolizes the cross lower back of slight and life to the world at the same time as Persephone is allowed to go to her mom on the ground, marking the converting seasons.

Poppy Flower: The poppy flower is associated with Demeter and her grief all through the time whilst Persephone is in the UnderworldIts vibrant color contrasts with the barrenness of the earth all through Demeter's mourning length.

Cornucopia (Horn of Plenty): Demeter is every now and then depicted maintaining a cornucopia, a photo of abundance and loadsIt reinforces her function because of the reality the organisation of bountiful harvests and agricultural prosperity.

Demeter's mythological trips

Demeter's mythological trips are regularly targeted around her quest to reunite at the side of her daughter, Persephone, who have become kidnapped through manner of HadesThese trips are vital to her person and the changing seasons in Greek mythologyHere are key moments from Demeter's mythological journeys:

The Abduction of Persephone:

The pivotal moment in Demeter's journey begins with the abduction of her daughter, Persephone, thru HadesThis occasion plunges Demeter into deep grief and melancholy, main to her look for Persephone.

Demeter's mythological journeys are often focused spherical her quest to reunite in conjunction with her daughter, Persephone, who became kidnapped through HadesThese journeys are critical to her character and the changing seasons in Greek mythologyHere are key moments from Demeter's mythological journeys:

The Abduction of Persephone:

The pivotal second in Demeter's journey begins offevolved with the kidnapping of her daughter, Persephone, by way of HadesThis event plunges Demeter into deep grief and melancholy, essential to her search for Persephone.

Encounter with Celeus and Metaneira:

While looking for Persephone, Demeter arrives in Eleusis and encounters Celeus and Metaneira, the king and queen of the placeShe assumes the guise of an antique woman and is taken into their domestic as a nurse for their son, DemophonThis come upon marks a turning factor in the fantasy.

Demeter's Gift of Immortality:

In gratitude for Celeus and Metaneira's hospitality, Demeter involves a preference to make Demophon immortalShe secretly locations the toddler inside the hearth every night time to burn away his mortality, but Metaneira discovers her movements and is horrified.

Reunion with Persephone:

Zeus intervenes to strong Persephone's skip once more from the UnderworldHades has the same opinion to launch her however cunningly gives her pomegranate seeds to consume, which bind her to the Underworld for a part of the yrWhen mother and daughter are in the long run reunited, Demeter's delight brings about the appearance of spring and the renewal of life in the international.

Creation of the Eleusinian Mysteries:

As a end stop end result of her memories in Eleusis, Demeter initiates the Eleusinian Mysteries, a series of secretive spiritual rites and ceremoniesThese mysteries promised initiates a deeper information of the cycles of life, death, and rebirth and held extremely good importance in historic Greek religion.

The Seasonal Cycle:

Demeter's annual reunion with Persephone and their separation inside the Underworld deliver an motive of the changing seasons in Greek mythologyDuring Persephone's absence in the Underworld, Demeter grieves and motives wintry weather and barrennessWhen they will be reunited, the earth flourishes with life in spring and summer season.

Demeter's Divine Influence:

Demeter's have an effect on over agriculture and fertility is plain in her adventureHer emotions and actions proper now effect the herbal worldwide, emphasizing the interconnectedness between the gods and the mortal realm.

Chapter 5: Athena Goddess of Wisdom and Warfare

In Greek mythology, Athena is one of the most great and revered goddesses within the pantheonShe is frequently related to knowledge, courage, warfare, approach, and severa craftsLet's find out her vicinity inside the pantheon, which consist of her parentage and siblings:

Parentage:

Athena's parentage is definitely precise a number of the Greek gods and goddessesShe is typically taken into consideration to be the daughter of Zeus, the king of the gods, and Metis, a Titaness diagnosed for her information and foxyAccording to fable, Zeus swallowed Metis while she have come to be pregnant with Athena due to the fact he were warned that any infant she bore may be extra effective than himAthena then supposedly sprang simply grown and armored from Zeus' forehead.

Siblings:

Ares: Ares is Athena's half-brother, as every are the children of ZeusWhile Athena represents strategic and disciplined battle, Ares embodies the extra brutal and chaotic elements of struggleThey often have conflicting interests and are now and again portrayed as competition.

Apollo: Apollo is also Athena's half of-brother, being the son of Zeus and LetoApollo is associated with the arts, tune, prophecy, and recovery, amongst exclusive subjectsAthena and Apollo each percentage pastimes in information and understanding, however they've specific spheres of have an effect on.

Artemis: Artemis is the dual sister of Apollo and because of this moreover Athena's 1/2 of-sisterShe is the goddess of the search, desolate tract, and childbirthLike Apollo, Artemis has her private awesome area, however she shares a few similarities with Athena in terms of independence and energy.

Athena's Role in the Pantheon:

Athena is frequently regarded due to the fact the purchaser goddess of Athens, the capital of GreeceShe changed into particularly valid and worshiped inside the path of ancient Greece, and her have an impact on extended to severa aspects of lifeHere are a number of her terrific roles and attributes inside the pantheon:

Goddess of Wisdom: Athena is normally identified for her data, intelligence, and strategic questioningShe is often depicted as a smart counselor and advertising and marketing representative to big gods and heroes.

Goddess of Warfare: While Ares represents the brute strain of warfare, Athena embodies strategic conflict and is taken into consideration a protector of warriorsShe turned into believed to guide heroes in conflict and provide them with the knowledge to make tactical options.

Goddess of Crafts: Athena is related to numerous crafts, collectively with weaving and potteryShe changed into visible because the purchaser of expert artisans and craftsmen, and he or she done a function in promoting the development of lifestyle and civilization.

Guardian of Athens: Athena modified into taken into consideration the parent and protector of the town of AthensAccording to fantasy, she acquired a competition with Poseidon to decide who may be the city's purchaser deity through gifting the Athenians an olive tree, symbolizing peace and prosperity.

Virgin Goddess: Athena is frequently referred to as a virgin goddess, emphasizing her independence and self-relianceShe is one of the few Olympian deities who did now not have many romantic entanglements or offspring.

Personality Traits:

Wisdom: Athena is famend for her information and intelligenceShe is frequently depicted as a rational and strategic philosopher who values know-how and foresightHer awareness is a key detail of her character and gadgets her aside from exceptional deities.

Courage and Strength: Athena possesses both physical and ethical courageShe isn't always pleasant a protector of warriors however additionally an exemplar of braveness herselfShe is concept for her electricity and fearlessness inside the face of challenges.

Independence: Athena is frequently referred to as a virgin goddess, emphasizing her independence and self-relianceUnlike many special Greek gods and goddesses, she does now not have severa romantic entanglements or rely upon others for her strength or identification.

Strategic Thinking: Athena is a maintain close strategist, and her movements are guided by using the usage of careful making plans and foresightShe values intelligence and method over impulsive moves, which aligns at the facet of her position as a goddess of battle.

Fairness and Justice: Athena is related to concepts of fairness and justiceShe is frequently seen as an independent decide in disputes maximum of the gods and mortals, upholding the concept of justice and ethical order.

Motivations:

Promoting Wisdom: Athena's primary motivation is to promote expertise and know-how among mortals and gods alikeShe seeks to encourage learning, intelligence, and rational wondering.

Protecting Heroes and Warriors: Athena is stimulated to shield and guide heroes and warriors in their endeavorsShe often assists mortal heroes by using presenting them with strategic recommendation and data to advantage their goals.

Preserving Civilization: As a goddess of crafts, Athena is caused to keep and decorate the humanities and civilizationShe encourages the improvement of way of existence, structure, and craftsmanship among mortals.

Defending Justice: Athena is induced to uphold justice and equity, making sure that disputes are resolved equitably and that moral order is maintained in each the divine and mortal nation-states.

Symbols:

Owl: The owl is in reality considered one of Athena's most famous symbolsIt represents records and intelligence and is regularly depicted with Athena in paintings and literatureThe owl's association with the goddess underscores her role as a consumer of expertise.

Aegis: Athena's defend or shielding cloak, called the Aegis, is frequently embellished with the pinnacle of the Gorgon MedusaIt symbolizes her protective and warlike hassle, presenting safety to the ones she favors.

Olive Tree: Athena is credited with gifting the olive tree to the town of Athens, making it a splendid image of peace and prosperityThe olive tree represents her function due to the fact the daddy or mom of Athens and her contributions to civilization

Helmet and Spear: As a goddess of battle, Athena is once in a while depicted with a helmet and spear, symbolizing her readiness for war and her function in guiding warriors.

Spindle and Distaff: These are symbols of Athena's association with crafts and domestic competenciesThey constitute her role as a goddess of weaving and particular crafts.

key moments from his mythological journeys

Birth of Athena:

Athena's starting is a essential 2d in her mythologyShe have become born surely grown and armored from the brow of her father, Zeus, after he swallowed her mom, MetisThis delivery myth symbolizes her knowledge and association with mind and method.

Contest with Poseidon:

One of the maximum famous reminiscences concerning Athena is her contest with Poseidon for the patronage of AthensThey each supplied gadgets to the town, and Athena supplied the olive tree, on the equal time as Poseidon gave a saltwater springAthena's gift, symbolizing peace and prosperity, won the city's desire, and he or she or he have emerge as its patron deityThis story illustrates her expertise and civic have an effect on.

Role inside the Trojan War:

Athena executed a good sized feature in the occasions of the Trojan WarShe supported the Greeks and particularly favored Odysseus, supporting him collectively together with her awareness and guidanceHer interventions in the war are depicted in Homer's "Iliad."

The Judgment of Paris:

Athena have become one of the three goddesses (collectively with Hera and Aphrodite) who sought the judgment of Paris, a Trojan prince, to decide the fairest among themParis chose Aphrodite after she promised him the love of the maximum lovely mortal girl, Helen of Troy, leading to the activities that induced the Trojan War.

ransformation of Arachne:

In a lesser-diagnosed tale, Athena converted a skilled weaver named Arachne right into a spider for her conceitedness and satisfactionThis story illustrates Athena's role as a goddess of craft and punishment for hubris.

Athena and Heracles:

Athena had a high-quality courting with the hero Heracles (Hercules)She aided him ultimately of his Twelve Labors and guided him on diverse sportsThis highlights her defensive and strategic components.

The Birth of Erichthonius:

Athena have become worried within the transport of Erichthonius, a mythical early king of AthensAccording to fantasy, she took care of the toddler Erichthonius, who changed into born from the Earth, and positioned him in a sacred disciplineThis tale underscores her shielding and nurturing capabilities.

Athena and Pallas:

In some variations of Greek mythology, Athena had a close to friend named Pallas, with whom she engaged in fightDuring their struggle, Athena by way of accident killed Pallas and later took her buddy's name as part of her personal, becoming Athena Parthenos (Athena the Virgin)This tale displays the martial problem of her character.

Apollo - God of Light, Music, and Healing

Apollo is a excellent parent in Greek mythology and one of the Olympian godsLet's explore his vicinity in the Greek pantheon, which include his parentage and siblings:

Parentage:

Apollo's parentage is fairly complicated, as he's the son of Zeus, the king of the gods, and Leto (Latona in Roman mythology), a TitanessLeto had a challenging time giving beginning to Apollo and his dual sister Artemis because of the truth she turn out to be pursued and persecuted thru the jealous goddess Hera, Zeus's wifeEventually, Leto placed secure haven at the island of Delos, wherein she gave delivery to Apollo and Artemis.

Siblings:

Artemis: Apollo's twin sister, Artemis, is likewise a prominent Olympian goddessShe is the goddess of the hunt, barren place, and childbirthThe twins shared a close to bond and were often depicted collectively in mythology.

Hermes: Hermes, the messenger god and the god of exchange, alternate, and tourists, is Apollo's half of-brotherBoth Apollo and Hermes are associated with guiding and shielding mortals in unique techniques, with Apollo offering steering in subjects of awareness and the humanities.

Dionysus: In some variations of Greek mythology, Apollo is the half of-brother of Dionysus, the god of wine, ecstasy, and revelryTheir contrasting personalities and domains (Apollo's affiliation with order and rationality, and Dionysus's connection to chaos and party) make for an interesting dynamic.

Apollo's Place in the Pantheon:

Apollo holds a huge and multifaceted feature within the Greek pantheon, and he's frequently considered one of the maximum influential Olympian godsHere are some elements of Apollo's place in Greek mythology:

God of the Sun: Apollo is regularly associated with the solar, even though he is not the number one sun god in Greek mythology (that characteristic belongs to Helios)He is related to the solar's moderate, which represents knowledge, enlightenment, and reality.

God of Music and the Arts: Apollo is renowned due to the fact the god of track, poetry, and the humanitiesHe is credited with inventing the lyre, a musical tool, and is frequently depicted gambling itApollo is also a client of the Muses, the goddesses of the humanities, who encourage creativity in mortals.

God of Healing: Apollo is concept for his affiliation with recovery and medicinal drugHe is regularly referred to as Apollo Medicus and is taken into consideration a god who can every inflict and treatment sicknessesHis son, Asclepius, is a famous healer in Greek mythology.

Oracle at Delphi: One of Apollo's maximum well-known roles changed into due to the fact the consumer deity of the Oracle at Delphi, wherein priestesses known as the Pythia brought prophetic messages from the godPeople from all over Greece consulted the Oracle for steerage on important picks.

Archer and Warrior: Apollo is likewise a professional archer and warriorHe is from time to time depicted with a bow and arrows, symbolizing his functionality to supply every sickness and recuperationHe performed a function in numerous myths and battles.

Prophecy and Truth: Apollo is related to truth and prophecyHis oracles have been pretty seemed for his or her accuracy, and Apollo himself end up considered a god who need to show hidden understanding and provide guidance.

Personality Traits:

Intellect: Apollo is often portrayed as a pretty clever and rational deityHe is related to data, expertise, and easy questioning, that is meditated in his characteristic because the god of prophecy and the arts.

Creativity: Apollo is a client of the humanities, in particular music, poetry, and the MusesHe is depicted as a progressive and progressive god, inspiring people to precise themselves via tune and poetry.

Courage: Apollo isn't always best a god of mind and the humanities but also a warriorHe is thought for his braveness and strength, which can be obvious in his characteristic as an archer and in numerous myths in which he defends the gods and mortals.

Healing: Apollo has a compassionate side, as he is related to recuperation and remedyHe is every so often called "Apollo Medicus" and is concept to have the power to both inflict and treatment illnesses.

Balance: Apollo represents a experience of stability and harmonyHe embodies the concept that understanding and creativity need to be balanced with rationality and order, selling a harmonious existence.

Motivations:

Promoting Knowledge: Apollo's primary motivation is to sell know-how, information, and enlightenmentHe evokes people to are searching out truth, whether thru the humanities, intellectual pursuits, or the steering of oracles.

Inspiring the Arts: Apollo is stimulated to inspire imaginitive expressionHe encourages mortals to discover track, poetry, and exceptional innovative endeavors, seeing the charge in self-expression and the cultivation of lifestyle.

Healing and Medicine: Apollo's motivation to heal stems from his desire to relieve struggling and preserve a experience of stability and properly-being among peopleHe is seen as a compassionate deity who cares for the health and welfare of mortals.

Maintaining Order: As a god related to rationality and order, Apollo is stimulated to keep a revel in of balance and harmony in the internationalThis consists of resolving conflicts, guiding humanity, and upholding ethical and moral requirements.

Symbols:

Lyre: The lyre is one in every of Apollo's maximum iconic symbolsHe is often depicted gambling this musical tool, symbolizing his patronage of song and the arts.

Laurel Wreath: Apollo is often depicted wearing a laurel wreath on his headThe laurel tree is sacred to him and represents victory, honor, and fulfillment.

Bow and Arrows: Apollo is a professional archer and is every so often depicted with a bow and arrows, symbolizing his function as a protector and warriorHis arrows may additionally need to deliver each illness and healing.

Sun Chariot: Apollo is now and again associated with a chariot that includes the solar all through the sky, even though this function is extra prominently attributed to the Titan god HeliosNevertheless, Apollo's connection to the solar underscores his affiliation with moderate and enlightenment.

Oracle at Delphi: The Oracle at Delphi, wherein prophetic messages were added via priestesses on behalf of Apollo, is a full-size symbol of his feature as a god of prophecy and fact.

Serpent: Apollo's symbol of a serpent or snake is associated with his role as a healer, as snakes had been visible as creatures of rebirth and transformation.

powers and areas of effect

Solar Powers: While no longer the number one solar god (that position belongs to Helios), Apollo is frequently associated with the sunHe is the god of mild and enlightenment, representing the highbrow and current factors of daytimeThis reference to the solar indicates his feature in illuminating the sector with know-how and truth.

Prophecy: Apollo is probably quality mentioned for his characteristic due to the fact the god of prophecyThe most famous oracle in historic Greece, the Oracle of Delphi, become committed to himPriestesses referred to as the Pythia brought prophetic messages on his behalfApollo's oracles were consulted through using kings, leaders, and those in search of steering and notion into their futures.

Music and the Arts: Apollo is the client god of song, poetry, and the humanitiesHe is credited with inventing the lyre and is regularly depicted gambling itHis divine have an impact on conjures up mortals to create tune, poetry, and works of paintingsThe Muses, who are his partners, characteristic muses to artists and poets.

Healing: Apollo is associated with recovery and medicationHe has the power to each inflict and remedy sicknesses, and he's sometimes called "Apollo Medicus." His son, Asclepius, is a renowned healer, and temples dedicated to Apollo frequently served as centers for clinical treatment and care.

Warrior and Protector: Apollo is a professional warrior who can wield a bow and arrows with extremely good precisionHe defends the gods and mortals in competition to severa threats, demonstrating his defensive traitsIn instances of catastrophe, he can unleash terrible arrows, symbolizing his electricity and authority.

Intellect and Wisdom: Apollo is a god of mind and records, selling rational wondering and easy-mindednessHe values information, purpose, and order, and he encourages mortals to are looking for reality and enlightenment.

Balance and Harmony: Apollo embodies a experience of stability and harmony within the internationalHe strives to keep equilibrium in every the natural and ethical orderThis includes resolving conflicts, upholding justice, and promoting moral behavior

Guidance for Heroes: Apollo frequently offers steering and help to mortal heroesHe aids them in their quests, imparting strategic advice and safetyNotable heroes like Perseus and Heracles received his help.

Cultural Development: Apollo is related to the improvement of way of life and civilizationHe encourages the cultivation of the arts, craftsmanship, and intellectual interests, contributing to the advancement of society.

Artemis is a wonderful goddess in Greek mythology, regarded for her affiliation with the search, desert, childbirth, and the moonLet's discover her location inside the Greek pantheon, which consist of her parentage and siblings:

Parentage:

Artemis is the daughter of Zeus, the king of the gods, and Leto (Latona in Roman mythology), a TitanessHer twin brother is Apollo, making her one of the few divine siblings who percentage a close bond in Greek mythologyArtemis and Apollo are taken into consideration the offspring of a sacred union among Zeus and Leto.

Siblings:

Apollo: As said earlier, Apollo is Artemis's twin brotherApollo is a distinguished Olympian god related to the sun, song, prophecy, restoration, and the artsThe bond among Artemis and Apollo is wonderful of their respective mythologies.

Artemis's Place within the Pantheon:

Artemis holds a totally specific and effective function in Greek mythology, and she or he or he's related to severa key factors of life and natureHere are a few important components of her vicinity inside the pantheon:

Goddess of the Hunt: Artemis is splendid known as the goddess of the questShe is frequently depicted with a bow and arrows and is taken into consideration the protector of untamed animalsArtemis and her nymph partners roamed the forests, demonstrating her prowess as a professional huntress.

Goddess of Wilderness: Artemis is cautiously linked to the untamed wasteland, symbolizing the unspoiled and wild factors of natureShe is a parent of the forests and mountains and is regularly invoked by way of these looking for to navigate the traumatic conditions of the herbal international.

Goddess of Childbirth: Artemis is also respected as a goddess of childbirth and protector of younger kids and girls in hard workIn this role, she contrasts at the facet of her brother Apollo, who can supply every illness and healing.

Mistress of Animals: Artemis's love for animals extends to her function as the protector of all dwelling creatures inside the wildShe is devoted to preserving the steadiness of nature and making sure the well-being of animals underneath her care.

Moon Goddess: Artemis has a connection to the moon, and he or she or he is every so often called the goddess of the moonlightIn this aspect, she is associated with the nighttime and the cycles of the moon.

Virgin Goddess: Similar to Athena, Artemis is regularly considered a virgin goddessShe is fiercely independent and bored with romantic relationships, who favor to interest on her very own pastimes and her characteristic as a dad or mum.

Moral and Ethical Standards: Artemis embodies a revel in of ethical and moral purityShe upholds strict codes of behavior, inclusive of chastity and righteousness, and punishes folks that transgress her values.

Personality Traits:

Independence: Artemis is fiercely impartial and values her autonomyShe is regularly depicted as a goddess who isn't always interested by romantic relationships and chooses to live a virgin, embodying the concept of self-sufficiency.

Protective: Artemis is fiercely shielding, especially of the natural international and its creaturesShe is thought for her sturdy sense of duty in safeguarding wild animals and ensuring the nicely-being of ladies at some point of childbirth.

Strong-Willed: Artemis is resolute and decided, whether or not or now not or not in her interests as a huntress or in her function as a protectorHer sturdy will and resolution are meditated in her unwavering dedication to her values.

Fearless and Assertive: As the goddess of the hunt, Artemis is brave and assertiveShe well-known braveness and tenacity on the equal time as monitoring and looking wild pastime, symbolizing her personal strength and resilience.

Moral and Just: Artemis upholds a strict ethical code and is idea for her enjoy of justiceShe punishes people who transgress her values, mainly in instances of immodesty or cruelty closer to animals.

Motivations:

Preserving Nature: Artemis's primary motivation is to shield and preserve the natural worldwideShe is a parent of the barren region and the animals that inhabit it, and he or she is deeply devoted to preserving the stableness and purity of the natural environment.

Protecting Women and Children: Artemis is also inspired thru her characteristic as a protector of ladies inside the route of childbirth and younger childrenShe guarantees their protection and well-being, symbolizing her compassion and nurturing aspect

Maintaining Virtue: Artemis is inspired to uphold moral and ethical virtues, consisting of chastity and righteousnessShe expects mortals to paste to those virtues and punishes people who violate them.

Chapter 6: God of War

The Greek god of conflict represents the brutal and violent factors of conflict, in assessment to his sister Athena, who embodies strategic and disciplined struggleLet's find out Ares's place in the Greek pantheon, which includes his parentage and siblings:

Parentage:

Ares is the son of Zeus, the king of the gods, and Hera, the queen of the godsHe is considered one of their many divine offspring and is considered one of the Olympian gods

Siblings:

Athena: Ares's sister Athena, regularly associated with information, braveness, and strategy, represents a contrasting element of struggleWhile Ares embodies the chaos and brutality of conflict, Athena emphasizes the rational and strategic elements of warfareThis evaluation often leads to opposition and struggle the numerous 2 siblings.

Apollo: Apollo is a few different half of-brother of Ares, being the son of Zeus and LetoApollo is understood for his affiliation with track, prophecy, and recuperation, making him pretty tremendous from the warlike Ares.

Artemis: Ares's sister Artemis is the goddess of the hunt, barren region, and childbirthShe, like Apollo, has pastimes and attributes that diverge appreciably from Ares's region of warfare.

Hermes: Hermes, the messenger god, is likewise a half of-brother of AresHe is related to trade, change, and tourists and possesses a completely unique set of attributes and duties.

Personality Traits:

Aggressive and Impulsive: Ares is idea for his competitive and impulsive natureHe revels within the chaos and violence of struggle and is regularly depicted as a warm-headed and fierce warrior.

Fearless: Ares embodies fearlessness and valor within the warmth of struggleHe evokes warriors to price into combat without hesitation, embracing the risks of conflict.

Brutal and Violent: Ares represents the brutal and violent additives of conflictHe relishes within the bloodshed and chaos of war, displaying little regard for the consequences or the nicely-being of those worried.

Lack of Strategy: Unlike his sister Athena, who represents strategic battle, Ares is often seen as lacking in strategic wonderingHis moves are pushed extra via a thirst for warfare and combat than with the aid of careful making plans.

Passionate: Ares is obsessed on struggle and the thrill of fightHis excessive emotions energy him to are looking for war and engage in bodily fight each time the possibility arises.

Motivations:

Love of War: Ares's primary motivation is his love of battle and the satisfaction of conflictHe seeks out possibilities to engage in combat and revels inside the chaos and violence that battle brings.

Desire for Glory: Ares is recommended with the aid of using the choice for glory and popularity at the battlefieldHe values the respect and status that consist of being a expert warrior and scary others to combat fearlessly.

Conflict and Strife: Ares is also inspired with the useful useful resource of his affinity for battle and strife He thrives in conditions of discord and chaos and is regularly associated with stirring up disputes and fueling conflicts.

Champion of Warriors: Ares sees himself as a champion of warriors and the embodiment of martial prowess He conjures up and protects folks who encompass the life of a soldier or warrior.

Symbols:

Spear and Shield: Ares is regularly depicted wielding a spear and guard, which is probably symbols of his function due to the reality the god of battle These guns constitute his martial prowess and readiness for warfare.

Helmet and Armor: He is every so often portrayed sporting a helmet and armor, emphasizing his recognition as a warrior god.

Vulture: In a few representations, the vulture is associated with Ares It is a scavenger hen that feeds on the remains of fallen infantrymen, symbolizing the aftermath of battle and the brutality of struggle.

Dogs: Ares is once in a while determined thru using dogs, in particular fierce and competitive onesThese animals reflect his private aggressive and combative nature.

Flaming Torch: Ares is every so often depicted preserving a flaming torch, which symbolizes the negative and fiery element of conflict.

Ares, the Greek god of warfare, powers

Enhanced Combat Skills: Ares has high-quality combat capabilities, making him a formidable warriorHe excels in hand-to-hand combat, swordplay, and the use of guns on the aspect of spears and shields.

Example: In Greek mythology, Ares frequently participates in battles alongside mortal warriors and can flip the tide of a warfare collectively together together with his extraordinary combat talents.

Battle Rage: Ares has the electricity to result in a frenzied war rage in mortals, developing their electricity, braveness, and ferocity in fightThis energy can be both a blessing and a curse, because it leads to accelerated violence on the battlefield

Example: During the Trojan War, Ares allows the Trojans, and his have an effect on spurs on their warriors, consisting of Hector, to combat with unrivaled bravery and aggression.

Invulnerability: Ares is normally depicted as being nearly invulnerable to mortal guns, making him difficult to harm in battleHis divine nature gives him a diploma of protection in competition to standard weaponry.

Example: In severa myths, Ares is wounded in war but rarely severely harmed or killed by using manner of mortal guns.

Shape-transferring: Ares can trade his form, allowing him to seem in severa guises on the battlefield or in distinctive conditionsThis capacity can be used for each tactical advantage and deception.

Example: In the myth of Ares and Aphrodite, he transforms into specific office work to break out the wrath of Hephaestus, Aphrodite's husband.

Fear Induction: Ares can instill fear inside the hearts of his enemies, weakening their remedy and inflicting panic on the battlefieldThis strength can demoralize opposing forces.

Example: In the "Iliad," Ares is said to inspire worry some of the Greek soldiers sooner or later of the Trojan War, developing chaos and confusion.

Teleportation: Ares can right away teleport himself to unique places, allowing him to appear on battlefields and conflicts wherever they may be taking area.

Example: In Greek mythology, Ares is regularly defined as rapid transferring from one battlefield to each extraordinary, assisting those who invoke his beneficial resource.

Protection of Warriors: Ares watches over and protects people who embody the lifestyles of a soldier or warriorHe can provide steerage, concept, and opt to parents which might be in search of his help in battle.

Example: In numerous myths and epic poems, Ares is invoked via heroes and warriors for his protection and assist of their navy endeavors.

Stirring Conflicts: Ares has the electricity to incite and intensify conflicts and disputes, not handiest in war but moreover in numerous elements of mortal lifeHe can gasoline discord and animosity amongst individuals and corporations.

Example: Ares's involvement in sparking conflicts is apparent in lots of Greek myths where disputes and wars are instigated through his affect.

big moments from Ares's mythological journeys:

Birth and Parentage:

Ares grow to be born to Zeus and Hera, making him one of the Olympian godsHis parentage gadgets the diploma for his feature because the god of war.

Affair with Aphrodite:

One of the most well-known tales regarding Ares is his affair with Aphrodite, the goddess of love and beauty, who become married to Hephaestus, the god of informationThis illicit dating emerge as discovered and uncovered, leading to scandal some of the gods and further illustrating Ares's impulsive nature.

Chapter 7: Aphrodite Goddess of Love and Beauty

Aphrodite, the Greek goddess of love, beauty, and desire, occupies a applicable location in the Greek pantheonLet's discover her function within the pantheon, together with her parentage and siblings:

Parentage:

Aphrodite's parentage varies in a single-of-a-type variations of Greek mythology, which offers to the complexity of her man or woman:

Hesiod's Theogony: In Hesiod's account, Aphrodite is born from the sea foam (aphros in Greek) that common while the severed genitals of Uranus (the sky) fell into the oceanThus, she has no mortal parentage and is considered one of the oldest Olympian deities.

Homer's Iliad: In Homer's epic poem, Aphrodite is depicted due to the fact the daughter of Zeus, the king of the gods, and Dione, a minor goddessThis version gives her as a more conventional divine offspring.

Siblings:

Aphrodite has severa 1/2 of-siblings a few of the Olympian godsSome of her superb siblings encompass:

Ares: Ares, the god of conflict, is truly certainly one of Aphrodite's maximum well-known siblingsDespite their contrasting domains, they're frequently associated with passionate love and choice.

Apollo: Apollo, the god of the solar, song, and prophecy, is some other half of-brother of AphroditeWhile their domains range, both are first rate deities within the Greek pantheon.

Artemis: Artemis, the goddess of the hunt and wilderness, is a half-sister to AphroditeThey represent opposing elements of femininity, with Aphrodite embodying love and beauty on the same time as Artemis personifies independence and the wild.

Hermes: Hermes, the messenger god, is likewise a sibling of AphroditeHis role is top notch from hers, specializing in conversation, trade, and adventure.

Aphrodite's Place in the Pantheon:

Aphrodite is a applicable parent in Greek mythology because of her area of affection, splendor, and preferenceHere are a few key factors of her location within the pantheon:

Goddess of Love and Desire: Aphrodite is at the entire referred to as the goddess of love and choiceShe personifies the romantic and sensual elements of human relationships and is regularly invoked in topics of affection and attraction.

Goddess of Beauty: Aphrodite is likewise related to bodily splendor and aesthetic attractionHer radiant splendor is frequently defined as top notch some of the gods and mortals.

Protector of Romantic Relationships: Aphrodite protects romantic relationships and marriagesShe is idea to have the power to inspire and nurture love among people.

Influence on Mortals: Aphrodite has a profound have an impact on on mortals, often entangling them inside the complexities of affection and desireHer capability to purpose love and ardour is a ordinary subject matter in Greek mythology.

Connection to the Sea: Aphrodite's shipping from the ocean foam links her to the ocean, and she or he or he is sometimes related to maritime factorsHer have an effect on over sailors and seafarers is also stated in some myths.

Cultural Significance: Aphrodite's have an impact on extends to numerous elements of ancient Greek manner of life, which include art work, poetry, and philosophy, wherein splendor and love had been huge troubles.

Cult Worship: Aphrodite modified into significantly worshiped for the duration of the Greek global, with cults and temples dedicated to her in numerous citiesHer worship finished a big function in Greek religious practices.

Aphrodite divine powers

Power of Attraction: Aphrodite possesses the capacity to encourage deep emotions of love, desire, and affection amongst both gods and mortalsHer divine have an effect on could make human beings irresistibly attractive to each other, growing passionate and romantic connections.

Example: In the parable of Pygmalion and Galatea, Aphrodite brings a statue to life because of the truth Pygmalion falls in love with itThis illustrates her electricity to imbue inanimate devices with beauty and life.

Matchmaking and Love Spells: Aphrodite has the energy to act as a matchmaker, bringing couples together and helping them conquer boundaries to their loveShe is regularly invoked with the useful resource of the usage of fans seeking her useful resource.

Example: In the tale of Eros (Cupid in Roman mythology) and Psyche, Aphrodite's involvement effects in a chain of trials and demanding situations designed to test the energy of Psyche's love for Eros.

Influence Over Marriage: Aphrodite protects and influences the group of marriageShe is related to the sanctity of marital bonds and the harmony among spouses.

Example: In Homer's "Iliad," Aphrodite intervenes to save Helen, who end up married to Menelaus, via manner of the usage of transporting her some distance from chance and lower returned to her husband.

Beauty and Physical Attractiveness: Aphrodite personifies bodily splendor and beautyHer very presence exudes an air of secrecy of fascinating enchantment.

Example: In the story of the "Judgment of Paris," Aphrodite is provided the golden apple for being the maximum lovable the various goddesses, a choice that outcomes inside the Trojan War.

Influence Over Desire: Aphrodite governs now not high-quality romantic love but additionally choice in a broader enjoyThis consists of passions, longings, and appetites, whether or now not or no longer they be for romance, splendor, or every different deeply felt craving.

Example: Aphrodite's affect extends to numerous types of preference, from romantic want to the pursuit of innovative splendor and creativity.

Representation of Sensuality: Aphrodite embodies sensuality and the pleasures of the sensesShe celebrates and promotes the amusement of bodily and emotional pleasures.

Example: The opposition of Aphrodisia, celebrated in honor of Aphrodite, blanketed feasts, song, dancing, and awesome sensual and thrilled sports activities sports.

Cultural and Artistic Influence: Aphrodite's first-class of beauty and love has had a profound effect on artwork, literature, and cultural beliefs all through records, inspiring artists, poets, and writers.

Example: In historic Greek art work and literature, Aphrodite's photo and issues associated with love and splendor had been usually depicted in numerous paperwork.

Symbols

The Dove:

Explanation: The dove is one of the maximum famous symbols of AphroditeIt represents love, peace, and beautyDoves were believed to be sacred to Aphrodite and have been often associated with her function due to the fact the goddess of affection and choice.

The Rose:

Explanation: The rose is a not unusual image of affection and splendorIt is intently related to Aphrodite's attributes, emphasizing her feature as the goddess of romantic and bodily loveRed roses, mainly, characterize passionate love.

The Scallop Shell:

Explanation: The scallop shell is a photo of Aphrodite's begin from the ocean foamAccording to mythology, she emerged actually grown from the ocean, and her beginning is often depicted at the side of her reputation in a scallop shellThis shell is a example of her connection to the ocean and her beginning.

The Myrtle Wreath:

Explanation: The myrtle wreath, crafted from the leaves and plant life of the myrtle plant, become worn via way of brides in historical Greece at some stage in marriage ceremony ceremoniesAphrodite's association with marriage and romantic love makes the myrtle wreath a photo of marital bliss and fertility.

The Mirror:

Explanation: Mirrors had been taken into consideration essential accessories in the historic global for reinforcing one's splendorAphrodite is regularly depicted searching proper into a mirror, signifying her association with physical look and the notion of self-love and self-care.

he Swan:

Explanation: Swans are smooth and stylish birds, and they characterize beauty, purity, and appealAphrodite is every so often related to swans, mainly in depictions of her starting from the ocean, wherein she might be surrounded thru swans.

The Apple:

Explanation: The apple, frequently related to Aphrodite's feature within the "Judgment of Paris" myth, represents desire and temptationIn the parable, she offers Paris the golden apple as a bribe to pick her because the most lovely most of the goddesses.

The Seashell Necklace:

Explanation: Aphrodite is every so often depicted wearing a necklace manufactured from seashells, reinforcing her connection to the sea and her beginning regionThis symbolizes her splendor, appeal, and attraction.

The Dolphin:

Explanation: Dolphins are seemed for his or her playful and happy natureThey also are associated with Aphrodite's begin from the seaDepictions of Aphrodite using inside the returned of a dolphin emphasize her connection to the sea and its inhabitants.

big moments from Aphrodite's mythological journeys:

Aphrodite's Birth:

According to one of the maximum famous myths, Aphrodite have turn out to be born from the sea foam close to the island of CyprusShe emerged absolutely grown and especially lovable from the foam, riding a shellThis fantasy emphasizes her affiliation with the ocean and her not possible to resist enchantment.

The Contest of the Golden Apple:

Aphrodite played a crucial position inside the Judgment of Paris, a contest that in the long run introduced at the Trojan WarShe, alongside thing Hera and Athena, sought the judgment of Prince Paris of Troy to decide who changed into the fairest goddessAphrodite received by manner of the usage of promising Paris the love of the most adorable mortal female, Helen of Sparta, which delivered about the activities leading to the Trojan War.

Aphrodite and Ares:

Aphrodite had a passionate affair with Ares, the god of warThis illicit dating highlighted her affiliation with choice and passionTheir union emerge as a photograph of the mingling of love and warfare.

Chapter 8: Hephaestus God of Blacksmiths and Fire

Hephaestus, the Greek god of knowledge, blacksmiths, and fireplace, occupies a unique location within the pantheon of Greek gods and goddessesHere's an exploration of Hephaestus's characteristic, parentage, and his relationships alongside collectively along with his divine siblings:

Parentage:

Hephaestus's parentage varies in top notch myths, but the most notably normal model states that he is the son of Zeus and Hera, the king and queen of the Olympian godsIn some bills, it's far advised that Hera gave start to Hephaestus without the involvement of Zeus, making him one of the unusual gods born from a unmarried parentThe times of his begin and his mother's moves in a while have giant implications for his individual and vicinity within the pantheon.

Physical Attributes:

Hephaestus is often depicted as a robust and bearded god, now and again with a limp because of a fall from Mount Olympus as a toddler, an occasion often attributed to Hera's rejection of himHe is also established with a hammer, anvil, or exceptional blacksmithing equipment, symbolizing his area over craftsmanship and fireside.

Role inside the Pantheon:

Hephaestus performs a vital feature in the Greek pantheon, in big as the god of information and eraHis abilties as a blacksmith and inventor are legendary, and he's chargeable for developing some of the gods' divine guns and artifacts, together with Zeus's thunderbolts, Athena's shield, and Achilles's armorHis position as a divine blacksmith aligns him with the mortal realm, as he crafts each divine and mortal devices, showcasing his versatility and creativity.

Siblings:

Hephaestus has severa divine siblings, as he is a part of the Olympian generation of godsSome of his outstanding siblings encompass:

Ares: Ares is the god of warfare and represents the extra brutal and chaotic factors of war, in assessment to Hephaestus's craftsmanship and ingenuity.

Athena: Athena is the goddess of understanding, strategy, and battleShe often collaborates with Hephaestus, using his creations for her skills, which includes her shield and armor.

Apollo and Artemis: Apollo is the god of the sun, tune, and prophecy, while Artemis is the goddess of the search and barren regionHephaestus's abilties may also have been used in crafting components in their domains, which includes Apollo's lyre and Artemis's looking gadget.

Hermes: Hermes is the messenger god and a trickster discern, diagnosed for his cunning and paceWhile their domain names are quite one-of-a-type, they percent a mischievous streak in some myths

Personality Traits:

Creativity and Ingenuity: Hephaestus is known for his amazing creativity and ingenuity as a blacksmith and craftsmanHe has the capability to convert uncooked substances into complicated and valuable artifacts, showcasing his innovative mind.

Resilience: Hephaestus's existence tale is marked with the useful resource of manner of adversity, as he became born with a deformity and modified into solid out of Olympus via his mom,HeraDespite those worrying situations, he indicates resilience and resolution in overcoming barriers.

Patience: Crafting complicated gadgets and working with hearth requires brilliant staying electricity, a trait Hephaestus possesses in abundanceHe can spend lengthy durations meticulously forging his creations.

Compassion: Hephaestus is frequently depicted as a compassionate and traumatic godHe is known for his kindness and willingness to help others, which incorporates mortals who're searching out his assistance or safety.

Forgiveness: Despite the mistreatment he persisted from some of the gods, Hephaestus is capable of forgivenessHe forgave his mom, Hera, for her rejection and even created lovely presents for her.

Motivations:

Pursuit of Excellence: Hephaestus is stimulated by using way of his choice to advantage excellence in craftsmanshipHe strives to create items of exceptional beauty and capability, regularly as items for the alternative gods.

Seeking Acceptance: One of Hephaestus's underlying motivations is the choice for attractiveness and reputation, specially from his circle of relatives and fellow godsDespite his deformity, he seeks to prove his genuinely well worth via his creations

Craftsmanship for the Greater Good: Hephaestus uses his competencies no longer exquisite for private pride but moreover for the extra precise of the gods and mortalsHe crafts divine guns and artifacts that beneficial aid in the protection of Olympus and the welfare of humanity.

Symbols:

Hammer and Anvil: The hammer and anvil are the maximum iconic symbols associated with

HephaestusThey represent his function as a blacksmith and his capability to forge gadgets with precision and know-how.

Tongs and Forge: These tools are frequently depicted along the hammer and anvil, emphasizing Hephaestus's mastery of the blacksmith's craft and the usage of fireside in his paintings.

Crane: In some depictions, Hephaestus is proven using a crane or is accompanied through this henThe crane symbolizes vigilance and watchfulness, characteristics associated with his craftsmanship.

Volcano: As the god of fireside, Hephaestus is every now and then related to volcanoes and their fiery eruptions.

Donkey: Hephaestus is from time to time depicted riding a donkey, symbolizing his adventure and resilience as he traveled the earth seeking out his rightful vicinity a number of the gods.

Powers

Master Blacksmith: Hephaestus is renowned due to the fact the grasp blacksmith of the godsHis divine power permits him to craft virtually any object with remarkable precision and expertiseHe forges now not best guns and armor for the gods but additionally elaborate earrings, automatons, and different mechanical devicesHis craftsmanship is unmatched among each gods and mortals.

Control over Fire: As the god of hearth, Hephaestus has the ability to control and manipulate flamesThis energy is critical for his blacksmithing, as he uses hearth to warm temperature and form metalsIt moreover underscores his connection to volcanic interest, in which molten lava and fireside are full-size.

Inventor and Engineer: Hephaestus's divine creativity extends to invention and engineeringHe is credited with growing numerous resourceful gadgets and automatons, together with the mechanical servant Talos and severa precise mechanical wondersThese upgrades showcase his amazing thoughts and modern spirit.

Divine Weapons and Artifacts: Hephaestus crafts divine weapons and artifacts for the opposite godsHis creations include Zeus's thunderbolts, Athena's defend (Aegis), Achilles's armor, and Hermes's winged sandalsThese gadgets are regularly imbued with magical homes that decorate the talents of their wielders.

Protection of Mortals: Hephaestus's have an effect on extends to mortal nation-states, in which he is considered the protector of blacksmiths, craftsmen, and artisansHe bestows concept and capability upon mortal artisans, assisting them of their art workIn this ability, he encourages the development of human civilization.

Creative Inspiration: Hephaestus inspires mortal artists and inventors to push the limits of their craftsHis divine have an impact on can spark creativity and innovation in human beings, driving upgrades in art, era, and craftsmanship.

Conflict Resolution: Hephaestus's effect isn't always limited to his craftHe has been acknowledged to mediate conflicts some of the gods, the use of his rational and diplomatic technique to reconcile disputesHis workshop on Olympus serves as a unbiased floor in which gods can come together for resolutions.

Artistic Expression: While more often than not associated with sensible craftsmanship, Hephaestus's creativity moreover extends to creative expressionHe can create beautiful and tricky works of artwork, reflecting his appreciation for every shape and feature.

large moments and activities associated with Hephaestus in Greek mythology:

The Fall from Olympus:

Hephaestus's story starts with a dramatic and poignant occasionAs a infant, he changed into born with a physical deformity, which numerous in one-of-a-kind debts of the mythUpon seeing his deformity, his mom, Hera, have become full of shame and angerIn her wrath, she threw Hephaestus from Mount Olympus, and he fell for an entire day and night time in advance than landing on the island of LemnosThis fall marked the start of his mythological journey.

Residence on Lemnos:

After his fall from Olympus, Hephaestus was taken in via the use of the use of the human beings of Lemnos, who raised and cared for himHephaestus grew up on this island, in which he developed his competencies as a blacksmithHe built his first workshop and started out out crafting wonderful works of paintings and ingenious innovations.

Return to Olympus:

Hephaestus in the long run placed his manner lower lower back to Olympus, way to the intervention of different gods, particularly DionysusIn a few variations of the myth,

Hephaestus returned to Olympus using a donkey or muleHis go back to the divine realm marked a full-size second of reconciliation together along with his own family and his reputation quo because the god of expertise a number of the Olympians.

Creation of Divine Artifacts:

Hephaestus's journeys inside his workshop on Olympus were packed with creative endeavorsHe strong severa divine artifacts, which include Zeus's thunderbolts, Athena's guard (Aegis), Achilles's armor, and Hermes's winged sandalsThese creations showcased his unequalled capabilities as a blacksmith and inventor.

Chapter 9: Hermes Messenger of the Gods

Hermes holds a wonderful and multifaceted characteristic within the Greek pantheon, characterized via his numerous attributes and dutiesHere's an exploration of Hermes's place inside the pantheon, collectively with his parentage and siblings:

Parentage:

Hermes is the son of Zeus, the king of the Olympian gods, and Maia, a nymph and one of the Pleiades, a hard and speedy of 7 sisters diagnosed for his or her splendorMaia gave begin to Hermes in a cave on Mount Cyllene in ArcadiaThis parentage establishes Hermes as one of the Olympian gods, and his birthplace contributes to his affiliation with transitions and limitations.

Attributes and Symbols:

Hermes is known for severa specific attributes and logos:

Winged Sandals (Talaria): Hermes is frequently depicted wearing winged sandals, which give him the capability to fly with first rate tempoThese sandals are a photograph of his swiftness and agility.

Winged Helmet (Petasos): His helmet is also decorated with wings, representing his capability to traverse geographical areas and talk between the divine and mortal worlds.

Caduceus: Hermes's most well-known image is the caduceus, a fixed of human beings with intertwined serpents and wings at the topThis workforce shows his feature as the messenger of the gods and is frequently associated with commerce, verbal exchange, and negotiation.

Pouch (Kerykeion): Hermes includes a pouch, which symbolizes his cunning and resourcefulnessHe makes use of this pouch to maintain numerous items, which includes the stolen livestock of Apollo in one in all his well-known myths.

Role in the Pantheon:

Hermes performs a various and crucial position inside the Greek pantheon:

Messenger of the Gods: Hermes is the primary messenger of the Olympian godsHe guarantees messages the various gods, allows communique with mortals, and publications souls to the afterlifeHis swiftness and agility make him the appropriate divine courier.

God of Boundaries and Transitions: Hermes is related to transitions and limitations, both physical and metaphysicalHe is the daddy or mother of vacationers and crossroads, making sure steady journeys and clean transitions.

Trickster and Thief: Hermes possesses a mischievous and clever element, often mission pranks and guidelinesOne of his most well-known feats grow to be stealing Apollo's livestock quick after his starting, showcasing his cunning nature.

Patron of Merchants and Commerce: Hermes is the customer deity of traders, buyers, and changeHis characteristic as the god of trade underscores his connection to limitations and transitions, as change frequently consists of crossing geographical and cultural borders.

Guide to the Underworld: Hermes has a huge function in guiding souls to the afterlifeHe escorts the deceased to the area of Hades and ensures their constant passage, making him a psychopomp.

Siblings:

Hermes has numerous divine siblings, for the reason that he's a member of the Olympian era of gods:

Aphrodite: Hermes's sister Aphrodite is the goddess of affection, beauty, and choiceWhile their domain names variety, every deities play influential roles in the realm of human emotions and relationships.

Apollo: Hermes's half-brother Apollo is the god of the solar, music, and prophecyDespite their variations, Hermes and Apollo have a nice opposition, as visible of their interactions in mythology.

Ares: Ares, the god of warfare, is every other sibling of HermesTheir domains and personalities are quite extraordinary, with Hermes representing worldwide circle of relatives individuals and communication in assessment to Ares's martial nature.

Athena: Athena, the goddess of understanding and conflict, is likewise a sibling of HermesThey once in a while collaborate in their roles as advisors and diplomats a number of the gods.

Powers and Abilities:

Messenger of the Gods: Hermes is in most cases known as the messenger of the Olympian godsHe has the brilliant functionality to transport with exceptional swiftness, often depicted carrying winged sandals and a winged helmet, which permit him to adventure most of the divine realm, the mortal international, and the Underworld swiftlyThis tempo and agility make him the precise messenger and mediator most of the gods.

Psychopomp: Hermes is accountable for guiding souls to the afterlifeAs a psychopomp, he escorts the deceased souls to the arena of Hades, ensuring their secure passage and transition to the underworldHis role in principal the souls of the departed displays his association with transitions and limitations among existence and absence of existence.

Guardian of Boundaries: Hermes is the protector of tourists, crossroads, and boundariesHe watches over those who journey, making sure their steady passage and the a achievement navigation of borders and crossroadsIn this feature, he safeguards transitions in each bodily and metaphysical nation-states.

Trickster and Deceiver: Hermes possesses a smart and mischievous natureHe often engages in pranks and guidelines, outwitting each gods and mortalsHis quick wondering and wit allow him to navigate various conditions, from time to time the use of deception to attain his dreams.

Patron of Commerce: Hermes is the client deity of buyers, customers, and alternateHe presides over agency transactions and lets in changeHis have an impact on on this vicinity underscores his connection to obstacles and transitions, as change regularly consists of crossing geographic and cultural borders.

Diplomacy and Negotiation: Hermes's characteristic due to the fact the messenger of the gods extends to worldwide relations and negotiationHe mediates disputes most of the Olympian deities, the usage of his eloquence and persuasive competencies to reap resolutions and hold concord on Mount Olympus.

Influence inside the Mythological World:

Communication and Information: Hermes's role as a messenger is crucial for the flow of data maximum of the gods and the various divine realm and the mortal worldHis have an effect on ensures that divine decrees, prophecies, and messages attain their meant recipients in a well timed way.

Guidance and Protection: Hermes's guardianship over vacationers and crossroads gives a feel of protection to the ones embarking on tripsHis presence offers protection and guidance throughout transitions and possibly perilous conditions.

Bridge Between Realms: Hermes serves as a bridge some of the divine and mortal worlds, connecting them via his communication and steerageThis connection reinforces the interdependence of the two geographical areas in Greek mythology.

Representation of Human Traits: Hermes embodies traits consisting of hobby, adaptability, cleverness, and the ability to navigate alternate and uncertaintyThese dispositions reflect additives of the human experience and resonate with mortals.

Cultural Significance: Hermes's have an effect on extends beyond mythology and into the cultural and ancient narratives of historic GreeceHe is frequently depicted in artwork, literature, and theater, serving as a photo of communication, exchange, and transitions.

key moments from Hermes's mythological journeys:

The Infant Trickster:

From his infancy, Hermes displayed his clever and mischievous natureOne of his earliest feats involved stealing Apollo's farm animals fast after his beginningTo keep away from detection, Hermes reversed the hooves of the livestock and made them walk backward, confounding Apollo at the same time as he attempted to tune the stolen herd.

Invention of the Lyre:

Hermes is credited with inventing the lyre, a musical deviceAccording to the myth, he created the primary lyre with the useful resource of attaching strings to a tortoise shellHermes then provided this tool to Apollo as a peace providing after the livestock incidentApollo have become so stimulated with the lyre that he gave Hermes the Caduceus, the well-known group of workers decorated with intertwined serpents.

Messenger of the Gods:

Hermes's most full-size position have become that of the messenger of the Olympian godsHis trips as a divine messenger concerned traveling the various divine realm, the mortal worldwide, and the UnderworldHe turn out to be liable for delivering messages and decrees, inclusive of those from his father, Zeus.

Guiding Souls to the Afterlife:

As a psychopomp, Hermes guided the souls of the deceased to the UnderworldHe would possibly lead them very well all through the boundary some of the residing and the vain, ensuring their transition to the afterlifeHis presence provided consolation and guarantee to those passing into the place of Hades.

Assisting Perseus:

Hermes aided the hero Perseus at some point of his quest to slay the Gorgon MedusaHe supplied Perseus with winged sandals and the Cap of Invisibility, allowing him to technique Medusa without being became to stoneThese gives had been instrumental in Perseus's a success mission.

Rescue of Ares and Aphrodite:

In one myth, Hermes got here to the aid of Ares and Aphrodite, who had been stuck in an embarrassing and compromising situation with the resource of the solar god, HeliosHermes intervened with the resource of the use of his clever wit to diffuse the situation and keep the respect of the 2 enthusiasts.

The Judgment of Paris:

Hermes performed a role inside the Judgment of Paris, a opposition that in the long run delivered approximately the Trojan WarHe emerge as tasked with escorting the three goddesses—Aphrodite, Hera, and Athena—to Paris for him to pick the most lovely among themParis's choice of Aphrodite, who promised him the affection of Helen of Troy, had profound consequences.

Chapter 10: Hades God of the Underworld

Hades, the Greek god of the Underworld, occupies a completely unique and solemn vicinity in the Greek pantheon Here's an exploration of Hades's feature, parentage, and his significance in the Olympian circle of relatives:

Parentage:

Hades is the son of Cronus and Rhea, making him a part of the second era of Olympian godsHis siblings embody Zeus, the king of the gods, and Poseidon, the god of the oceanTogether, Zeus, Poseidon, and Hades divided the geographical regions of the area, with Zeus ruling the heavens, Poseidon governing the seas, and Hades presiding over the Underworld.

Role inside the Pantheon:

Hades's characteristic and region are outstanding from the ones of his brothers and considered one of a kind Olympian gods:

God of the Underworld: Hades is the ruler and god of the Underworld, referred to as the sector of the uselessHis number one duty is to supervise the souls of the deceased and preserve order in the afterlifeThis function sets him apart from the opportunity Olympians, who govern diverse additives of the mortal and divine worlds.

Guardian of the Dead: Hades is the parent of the souls of the departed, ensuring they obtain the Underworld after demiseHe judges the souls and determines their destiny, with the assist of judges like Minos, Rhadamanthus, and Aeacus.

Wealth and Resources: Hades's area consists of the massive wealth of the earth's subterranean nation-states, such as treasured metals and gemstonesAs a give up cease result, he is every now and then referred to as "Pluto," this means that that "wealth" or "riches."

Marriage to Persephone: Hades is also recounted for his abduction and marriage to Persephone, the daughter of Demeter, the goddess of agricultureThis union performs a vast characteristic inside the converting of the seasons, as Persephone spends a part of the 365 days with Hades in the Underworld, leading to the barren wintry climate months.

Symbols

Hades is associated with several symbols and attributes that represent his function due to the fact the ruler of the Underworld:

Cerberus: Cerberus is a 3-headed, massive dog that guards the entrance to the UnderworldIt prevents the residing from stepping into and the useless from escaping.

Bident: Hades regularly wields a -pronged workforce known as a bident, symbolizing his electricity and authority over the Underworld.

Helmet of Invisibility: Hades possesses a helmet that gives him invisibility, permitting him to move approximately undetected even as he wishes.

Key: He is sometimes depicted retaining a key, symbolizing his control over the doorway to the Underworld.

Powers

Ruler of the Underworld: Hades's primary divine strength is his dominion over the Underworld, the location of the vainHe governs this extraordinary and complicated realm, overseeing the souls of the deceased and keeping order amongst them.

Judgment of Souls: Hades has the authority to decide the souls of the departed, identifying their remaining fate within the afterlifeHe judges the deeds and moves of each soul, assigning them to precise regions of the Underworld primarily based on their conduct in lifestyles.

Invisibility: Hades possesses a helmet of invisibility, which offers him the energy to emerge as unseen at the identical time as he wears itThis potential permits him to transport approximately disregarded at the same time as he wishes to engage with the residing or the divine.

Control Over the Afterlife: Hades controls the cycle of shipping, life, and demiseHe oversees the transition of souls from the mortal international to the Underworld and ensures that they may be nicely cared for and judged in the afterlife.

Influence within the Mythological World:

Guardian of the Dead: Hades performs a essential position because the determine of the souls of the deceasedHis have an impact on extends to all mortals, as truely anyone need to in the long run bypass thru his realmThis concept reinforces the Greeks' statistics of the inevitability of lack of lifestyles.

Justice and Accountability: Hades's feature due to the fact the decide of souls promotes the idea of moral obligationHis judgments are based at the deeds and options of humans sooner or later of their lives, reinforcing the Greek belief inside the effects of one's actions.

Changing of the Seasons: Hades's marriage to Persephone, the daughter of Demeter, performs a position in the changing of the seasons in Greek mythologyWhen Persephone is with Hades inside the Underworld, Demeter mourns, principal to winterHer go back to the mortal global within the spring brings approximately the rebirth of vegetation and the onset of spring and summer season.

Cerberus and the Afterlife Barrier: Hades's three-headed dog, Cerberus, guards the entrance to the Underworld, preventing the residing from entering and the vain from escapingThis function reinforces the boundary between the realms of the residing and the useless.

Offerings and Rituals: In Greek manner of life, offerings and rituals had been made to Hades to are searching for his prefer and make certain a peaceful transition to the afterlifeThese practices highlighted the belief within the significance of honoring the lifeless and paying respects to Hades.

key moments and myths

Abduction of Persephone: One of the most well-known myths concerning Hades is the abduction of Persephone, the daughter of Demeter, the goddess of agricultureHades fell in love with Persephone and, with the consent of Zeus, abducted her and brought her to the UnderworldThis act brought about a duration of mourning and infertility on Earth as Demeter grieved the lack of her daughterEventually, a compromise turned into reached, permitting Persephone to spend a part of the three hundred and sixty five days collectively with her mother on Earth, fundamental to the converting of the seasons.

Encounter with Orpheus: Orpheus, a famend musician and poet, descended into the Underworld in an try to rescue his cherished partner, Eurydice, who had diedHades end up moved through manner of Orpheus's tune and agreed to permit Eurydice to move once more to the area of the dwelling, however with one situation: Orpheus want to now not appearance again at her until they every reached the groundUnfortunately, Orpheus couldn't withstand the temptation and appeared decrease once more, losing Eurydice all of the time.

Theseus and Pirithous: Theseus, a hero, and Pirithous, a fellow adventurer, attempted to abduct Persephone from the Underworld to marry herThey have been captured by way of the usage of Hades and chained to a rock inside the UnderworldHeracles (Hercules) sooner or later rescued Theseus, but Pirithous remained in the Underworld as punishment for his audacious act.

Heracles' Twelve Labors: In one among his labors, Heracles end up tasked with capturing the 3-headed dog Cerberus, who guarded the doorway to the UnderworldHeracles entered the vicinity of Hades, wrestled Cerberus into

Judgment of Souls: Hades become responsible for judging the souls of the deceased and assigning them to their suitable places in the UnderworldThis ongoing responsibility concerned interacting with the souls of mortals and overseeing the numerous areas of the Underworld, collectively with the Elysian Fields for the virtuous and the

Tartarus for the depraved.Submission, and taken him to the floor

After showing his strength, Heracles decrease once more Cerberus to Hades

While Hades is not stated for embarking on epic journeys like some distinct Greek deities and heroes, his realm inside the Underworld and his interactions with other gods and mortals played a essential characteristic in Greek mythologyThe myths surrounding him frequently cope with troubles of loss of life, the afterlife, and the results of human actions, making Hades a essential decide in knowledge the Greek view of mortality and the divine.

Dionysus - God of Wine and Celebration

Dionysus, the Greek god of wine, revelry, ecstasy, and the theater, occupies a completely precise and complex region in the Greek pantheonHis characteristic and attributes set him other than the alternative

Olympian godsHere's an exploration of Dionysus's location inside the pantheon:

Parentage:

Dionysus's parentage varies in specific myths, however the most often not unusual version identifies him because of the reality the son of Zeus, the king of the gods, and Semele, a mortal girlThis combined parentage places him in the 2d generation of Olympian godsHis beginning was unusual, as Zeus rescued him from his mom's womb after she became incinerated through his divine lightning bolts.

Attributes and Symbols:

Dionysus is characterized with the beneficial useful resource of numerous attributes and symbols that constitute his vicinity and person:

Thyrsus: Dionysus is frequently depicted keeping a thyrsus, a set of people adorned with ivy and a pineconeThe thyrsus symbolizes his connection to the natural worldwide and the vine, representing the dual nature of his region—ecstasy and transformation.

Grapes and Wine: Grapes and wine are essential symbols of DionysusHe is the god of viticulture (grape cultivation) and winemaking, emphasizing his association with revelry and intoxication.

Ivy and Panther: Dionysus is frequently located via ivy, it really is associated with his gala's and the Dionysian revelsHe is also now and again seen the usage of a panther, which represents his wild and unpredictable nature.

Theater Masks: Dionysus is considered the customer god of the theaterTheater masks, mainly the comedy and tragedy mask, are related to him, reflecting his feature in every lighthearted and dramatic celebrations.

Role inside the Pantheon:

God of Ecstasy and Revelry: Dionysus is the god of ecstasy, liberation, and revelryHis worship worried ecstatic rituals, song, dance, and the consumption of wine, frequently vital to a country of frenzied pride and modified attentionHis have an impact on turned into seen as transformative, offering an get away from the normal.

Nature Deity: Dionysus is carefully tied to the cycles of nature, mainly the increase of the grapevine and the production of wineHe represents the fertile and generative forces of the earth and the cyclical rebirth of life.

Bringer of Wine and Joy: Dionysus is credited with introducing the cultivation of grapes and the art work of winemaking to humanityWine, in Greek subculture, changed into a picture of pleasure, delight, and social birthday celebration, reflecting Dionysus's impact on Greek existence.

Theater and Art: Dionysus performed a pivotal role within the development of Greek theater, specifically tragedy and comedyThe theater modified into considered a sacred area for his worship, and his gala's, which encompass the Dionysia, featured dramatic performances that explored profound problem subjects.

God of Transformation: Dionysus represents the concept of transformation and trade, each in terms of private boom and the cycle of life and deathHe embodies the dualities of delight and sorrow, life and demise, and civilization and wilderness.

Fertility and Regeneration: As a nature deity, Dionysus have come to be associated with the regeneration of existence and the earth's fertilityHis worship frequently blanketed rituals alleged to make certain bountiful harvests.

Powers

Wine and Viticulture: Dionysus has mastery over the cultivation of grapes and the artwork of winemakingHe can promote the growth of grapevines, ensuring a bountiful harvestWine isn't pleasant a image of delight however additionally a technique via which Dionysus can bring about ecstasy and changed states of recognition.

Ecstasy and Transformation: Dionysus is associated with ecstasy and liberation from societal normsHis revels and rituals frequently incorporate music, dance, and the intake of wine, most critical individuals to a rustic of euphoria and modified recognitionHe represents the transformative power of these studies, in which people can in short escape the limitations of ordinary lifestyles.

Theater and Performance: Dionysus is the purchaser god of the theater, in particular tragedy and comedyHe conjures up creativity and imaginative expressionThe theater grow to be taken into consideration a sacred place for his worship, and his fairs featured dramatic performances that explored profound problem subjects, reflecting the dualities of lifestyles.

Natural Forces: As a deity linked to the cycles of nature, Dionysus embodies the fertility of the earth and the renewal of existenceHe represents the cyclical nature of the seasons, with the growth of grapes and the manufacturing of wine symbolizing regeneration and the eternal cycle of lifestyles.

Transgression of Boundaries: Dionysus is regularly associated with crossing boundaries and blurring the traces amongst oppositesHe challenges traditional norms, which includes the ones of gender and social orderHis worship encourages the breaking of societal taboos and conventions.

Influence inside the Mythological World:

Celebration and Joy: Dionysus's have an effect on is most prominently felt in celebrations and festivals committed to himThese sports were characterised thru exuberant festivities, music, dance, and the consumption of wine, permitting people to enjoy pleasure and a temporary launch from everyday problems.

Personal Transformation: Dionysus gives the potential for non-public transformation and self-discovery via the ecstatic and freeing stories associated with his worshipThese stories were visible as a manner of connecting with the divine and transcending everyday life.

Cultural and Artistic Legacy: Dionysus's patronage of the theater has left a protracted lasting legacy in the international of acting artsGreek tragedies and comedies, stimulated via his fairs, explored profound philosophical and moral questions and hold to steer theater and literature to at the prevailing time.

Religious Mysteries: Dionysus's worship changed into frequently shrouded in mystery, with initiates participating in mystery rituals known as the "Dionysian Mysteries." These rituals aimed to deepen participants' expertise of lifestyles, death, and the divine.

Social and Cultural Impact: Dionysus's have an effect on prolonged past spiritual and resourceful geographical areas into Greek societyHis gala's and rituals bolstered the importance of network, celebration, and the popularity of trade and transformation.

key moments from Dionysus's mythological trips:µ

Birth and Rescue from Semele's Womb:

Dionysus's myth starts offevolved offevolved with the fantastic times of his beginningHis mother, Semele, become a mortal girl who have become pregnant by means of the usage of way of Zeus, the king of the godsHera, Zeus's jealous companion, tricked Semele into asking Zeus to show his actual divine form, which brought about her being incinerated by Zeus's lightning boltsTo keep the unborn Dionysus, Zeus sewed him into his thigh until he became prepared to be bornThis specific transport emphasized his twin nature as every mortal and divine.

Education thru manner of Silenus:

Dionysus was entrusted to the care of Silenus, a smart and drunken satyr, who taught him approximately the cultivation of grapes and the art of winemakingDionysus may additionally later use this information to spread the cultivation of grapes and the manufacturing of wine.

Transformation of Pirates:

In one fable, Dionysus become captured via a set of pirates who deliberate to promote him into slaveryHowever, Dionysus revealed his divine nature thru turning the supply's rigging into vines and filling the deliver with wineThe organization went mad and leaped overboard, reworking into dolphinsThis fable showcases Dionysus's strength to spark off insanity and his capability to convert folks that defy him.

The Conquest of India:

Dionysus is frequently associated with trips to the East, together with the conquest of IndiaIn this mythological adventure, Dionysus led a advertising and advertising advertising marketing campaign to triumph over the lands of the East and unfold his worshipAlong the manner, he encountered various demanding situations and adventures, demonstrating his divine authority.

The Myth of Pentheus:

One of the most famous myths regarding Dionysus is his clash with King Pentheus of ThebesPentheus resisted the worship of Dionysus and attempted to suppress his fanaticsIn reaction, Dionysus added on Pentheus to go mad and be torn aside with the resource of his personal mom and aunts, who had been beneath the god's intoxicating have an impact onThis tale serves as a cautionary tale approximately the consequences of denying Dionysus's divinity.

Return to Olympus:

Despite his tumultuous trips and encounters with mortals, Dionysus in the end again to Mount Olympus as one of the Olympian godsHis vicinity maximum of the divine pantheon solidified his repute because the god of wine, revelry, and transformation.

Dionysus's mythological trips spotlight his twin nature as a god who brings every pride and madnessHis recollections emphasize the transformative power of his worship, the party of lifestyles, and the blurred barriers many of the normal and the divineDionysus's mythology remains a supply of concept in literature, art work, and manner of life, reflecting the long-lasting fascination along collectively with his multifaceted person.

Chapter 11: The Origins of Greek Mythology

In the sunrise of time, earlier than the world as we apprehend it came into life, there has been Chaos—a giant, formless void that enveloped the whole thing. From this primordial chaos, the very essence of advent emerged, giving beginning to the primary beings in Greek mythology.

Creation Myths

The historical Greeks, like many cultures at some point of information, sought to offer an cause at the back of the origins of the world and the universe through myths and recollections. These advent myths supplied a basis for know-how the natural global and humanity's location interior it.

One of the maximum enduring creation myths in Greek mythology tells of Gaia, the Earth, who emerged from Chaos and gave beginning to Uranus, the Sky. These primordial beings then delivered forth the Titans, powerful and historical deities who embodied herbal forces collectively with the earth, the sky, and the sea. The Titans, in turn, gave upward thrust to the Cyclopes and the Hecatonchires—massive beings with super power.

The Titans and Primordial Deities

The Titans completed a crucial characteristic within the early cosmogony of Greek mythology. Cronus, one of the Titans, overthrew his father Uranus and characteristic end up the ruler of the universe. However, Cronus end up destined to be overthrown thru the use of his very non-public son, Zeus, in a dramatic conflict that would shape the destiny of the Greek pantheon.

Among the Titans were moreover beings like Oceanus, the personification of the arena's oceans, and Rhea, the mom of Zeus and his siblings. These primordial deities represented the crucial elements of the cosmos and the herbal forces that dominated the vicinity.

The Birth of the Olympians

The overthrow of Cronus with the aid of Zeus marked the upward thrust of a current technology of gods—the Olympians. These twelve powerful deities, residing on Mount Olympus, ought to come to dominate Greek mythology. Zeus, the king of the gods, ruled alongside his siblings and fellow Olympians, alongside facet Hera, Poseidon, Demeter, Athena, Apollo, Artemis, Ares, Hephaestus, Aphrodite, Hermes, and Dionysus.

The myth of the shipping of Athena, who emerged without a doubt grown and armored from the top of Zeus, is a testomony to the innovative and symbolic nature of Greek mythology. Each of the Olympian gods and goddesses possessed outstanding personalities, domain names, and roles inside the divine hierarchy, reflecting the multifaceted nature of the sector they represented.

As we delve deeper into Greek mythology, we're able to come across those Olympian deities and explore their stories, personalities, and interactions with each mortals and distinctive gods. We will witness the drama in their conflicts, the intrigues of their relationships, and the enduring legacy they have left on the arena of literature, artwork, and culture.

But our journey does not cease here. The origins of Greek mythology are sincerely the begin—a prologue to a huge and problematic narrative so that it will take us on a fascinating exploration of a worldwide in which gods and mortals collide, in which heroes rise and fall, and wherein the human revel in is woven into the very cloth of the cosmos.

The Olympian Gods and Goddesses

The pantheon of Greek mythology is a grand meeting of deities, each with their very very personal precise attributes, personalities, and domains. As we delve deeper into this mythic realm, we encounter the Olympian gods and goddesses—the divine rulers of the cosmos and the important figures in Greek mythology.

Zeus: King of the Gods

At the pinnacle of Mount Olympus, Zeus, the thunderbolt-wielding king of the gods, reigns very excellent. His dominion extends over the sky, the heavens, and the jail tips that govern the universe. Zeus is not quality the ruler of gods but additionally the arbiter of justice and the protector of oaths and hospitality. His symbols include the lightning bolt and the eagle, and his authority is unquestioned a few of the gods.

Hera: Queen of the Gods

By Zeus's facet stands Hera, his sister and queen of the gods. Hera embodies the thoughts of marriage, own family, and constancy. She is often depicted as a regal decide, sporting a crown and defensive a pomegranate—a symbol of fertility. However, her relationship with Zeus is marked by means of the use of jealousy and conflicts, as

Zeus's severa infidelities test her staying strength and clear up.

Poseidon: God of the Sea

Poseidon, the strong god of the sea, commands the waters and the creatures that live under them. He wields a trident, a weapon that could shake the very foundations of the earth, and his have an impact on extends to earthquakes and storms. As the brother of Zeus and Hades, Poseidon plays a pivotal role in the divine triumvirate.

Demeter: Goddess of Agriculture

Demeter, the goddess of agriculture and the harvest, is responsible for the fertility of the land. Her association with the changing seasons is contemplated in the myth of her daughter, Persephone, who spends a part of the yr in the underworld with Hades. Demeter's grief inside the route of her daughter's absence consequences in the barren wintry climate months.

Athena: Goddess of Wisdom

Athena, the sensible and strategic goddess of information, is frequently depicted sporting a helmet and wearing a protect and spear. She is the client deity of Athens and a symbol of rational idea, method, and warfare. Athena's start, rising truly grown from the top of Zeus, underscores her unique popularity some of the Olympians.

Apollo: God of the Sun and Arts

Apollo, the radiant god of the solar, is a multifaceted deity related to track, poetry, prophecy, and recovery. He is regularly depicted with a lyre and the laurel wreath, symbols of inventive and highbrow achievement. The Oracle of Delphi, devoted to Apollo, served as a respected center of prophecy in the ancient global.

Artemis: Goddess of the Hunt

Artemis, Apollo's dual sister, is the goddess of the quest, barren region, and childbirth. She is often depicted with a bow and arrow, and her affinity for the herbal international is pondered in her feature as protector of animals and the wild. Artemis's association with the moon links her to the cycles of nature.

Ares: God of War

Ares, the god of conflict, represents the brutal and unfavorable elements of struggle. Unlike Athena, who embodies approach and tactical battle, Ares revels within the chaos of warfare and bloodshed. He is frequently portrayed as impulsive and reckless, a pressure of primal violence.

Hephaestus: God of Fire and Smithing

Hephaestus, the god of hearth and craftsmanship, is a professional blacksmith who forges the divine guns and artifacts of the gods. Despite his bodily deformity, he is extensively official for his progressive talents. Hephaestus's forge is placed beneath Mount Olympus, in which he tirelessly works to craft masterpieces.

Aphrodite: Goddess of Love and Beauty

Aphrodite, the goddess of love and splendor, embodies the appeal and ardour of romantic appeal. Her start is steeped in fable, springing up from the ocean foam near the island of Cyprus. Aphrodite's have an impact on extends old flame, encompassing the concept of physical and emotional splendor.

Hermes: Messenger of the Gods

Hermes, the fleet-footed messenger of the gods, is a multifaceted deity associated with tour, commerce, and cunning. He is regularly depicted with winged sandals and a caduceus, a hard and fast of employees entwined with serpents. Hermes serves as a bridge a number of the divine and mortal geographical regions, guiding souls to the underworld and facilitating verbal exchange most of the gods.

Dionysus: God of Wine and Revelry

Dionysus, the god of wine, ecstasy, and revelry, personifies the joyous and freeing elements of existence. His cult celebrates the intoxicating energy of wine and the transcendence it brings. Dionysus's myths regularly contain wild and ecstatic rites, contrasting with the more staid elements of the Olympian pantheon.

Hades: God of the Underworld

Hades, the lord of the underworld, recommendations over the world of the useless. His nation is a shadowy and mysterious place, wherein the souls of the deceased embark on their eternal adventure. Hades is a god of every fear and necessity, overseeing the stableness amongst life and dying.

These are the Olympian gods and goddesses who preside over the mythic landscape of Greek mythology. Their testimonies are as numerous and complicated because of the reality the human revel in itself, and they hold to captivate our imagination and offer insights into the complexities of the human scenario.

In the chapters that look at, we are able to discover the lives, myths, and interactions of these divine figures, witnessing their triumphs and trials, their passions and conflicts, and the long-lasting impact they have got had on the world of delusion, paintings, and lifestyle.

Chapter 12: Heroes and Heroines

The heroes and heroines of Greek mythology occupy a unique place within the collective creativeness. These huge-than-life figures embark on epic quests, confront bold demanding conditions, and embody the ideals and flaws of humanity. Their recollections resonate with us due to the truth they reflect the struggles, aspirations, and triumphs which can be part of the human experience.

The Heroic Quest

The concept of the hero's adventure is a routine subject matter in Greek mythology. Heroes are regularly known as upon to adopt incredible adventures, handling a series of trials and tests that in the end result in non-public boom and transformation. The hero's journey is a story structure that has stimulated endless tales during cultures and time periods.

Perseus and the Gorgon Medusa

One of the most famous Greek heroes, Perseus, was born under first rate instances. His mother, Danaë, have become imprisoned through her father, King Acrisius, due to a prophecy that her son ought to in the end kill him. However, the gods intervened, and Perseus turned into conceived at the same time as Zeus visited Danaë as a shower of golden rain.

Perseus's maximum renowned quest come to be to slay the Gorgon Medusa, a superb creature with snakes for hair whose gaze grew to become humans to stone. Armed with a reflective protect, winged sandals, and a paranormal sword, Perseus ventured into the perilous lair of Medusa and in the long run triumphed, the use of her severed head as a weapon.

Heracles (Hercules): A Hero's Trials

Heracles, known as Hercules in Roman mythology, is likely the maximum celebrated of all Greek heroes. His legendary power and staying power allowed him to undertake a sequence of twelve labors as punishment for a in shape of madness because of the goddess Hera. These labors blanketed slaying the Nemean Lion, taking photographs the Erymanthian Boar, and cleansing the Augean Stables, amongst others.

Heracles's journey turn out to be one of redemption and atonement, as he sought to show his worthiness and overcome his flaws. His labors have end up emblematic of the hero's quest for self-discovery and the triumph of virtue over adversity.

Jason and the Quest for the Golden Fleece

The story of Jason and the Argonauts is every other mythical story of heroism and adventure. Jason, the rightful heir to the throne of Iolchus, released right into a risky journey to retrieve the Golden Fleece, a image of kingship. He assembled a group of heroes referred to as the Argonauts and sailed aboard the deliver Argo to far flung lands, encountering numerous annoying situations and adversaries, alongside facet the sorceress Medea.

Jason's quest for the Golden Fleece symbolizes the hero's journey to benefit a noble intention, the help of supernatural allies, and the eventual achievement of destiny.

Theseus: Slayer of the Minotaur

In the coronary heart of ancient Crete, a large creature known as the Minotaur, 1/2-man and 1/2-bull, dwelled inside the labyrinthine palace of King Minos. Theseus, a hero diagnosed for his wit and bravado, volunteered to go into the labyrinth and defeat the Minotaur. Guided through the use of the love of Princess Ariadne and armed with a sword and a ball of thread, Theseus effectively navigated the labyrinth and slew the Minotaur, making sure the protection of his fellow Athenians.

The tale of Theseus represents the triumph of braveness and cunning over insurmountable odds, as well as the hero's responsibility to protect and hold his humans.

The Trojan War and the Heroes of the Iliad

The Trojan War, immortalized in Homer's epic poem, the "Iliad," is one of the maximum famous events in Greek mythology. The battle emerge as sparked with the aid of the kidnapping of Helen, the maximum lovable woman in the worldwide, with the useful resource of Paris, a Trojan prince. The Greek heroes, which includes Achilles, Odysseus, Agamemnon, and Ajax, rallied to rescue Helen and lay siege to the metropolis of Troy.

Achilles, the remarkable Greek warrior, became mentioned for his invulnerability—besides for his heel, the Achilles' heel, that may show to be his fatal weak factor. His internal conflict among honor and mortality office work a relevant subject matter within the "Iliad."

The "Iliad" is a effective exploration of the price of warfare, the hubris of heroes, and the inexorable impact of fate.

The Adventures of Odysseus

Following the sports of the Trojan War, the hero Odysseus released into an extended and hard journey home to Ithaca. His ten-year odyssey, chronicled in Homer's "Odyssey," is a testomony to wit, foxy, and perseverance.

Odysseus confronted severa trials and boundaries, which incorporates encounters with mythical creatures similar to the Cyclops Polyphemus, the sorceress Circe, and the sirens who lured sailors to their doom. His very last pass back domestic changed into a triumph of intelligence and resourcefulness, exemplifying the hero's quest to overcome adversity.

The Tragic Hero: Oedipus and Antigone

Greek mythology isn't always simplest replete with powerful heroes but moreover tragic figures whose memories feature cautionary stories. Oedipus, the king of Thebes, is one such tragic hero. Unknowingly, he fulfilled a prophecy that foretold he may kill his father and marry his mother. When he determined the reality, Oedipus blinded himself in horror and disgrace.

Oedipus's daughter, Antigone, is another tragic figure. Faced with the selection of obeying the law or honoring her brother's burial rights, she chose familial obligation over the edicts of the u . S . A ., ultimately most important to her tragic destiny.

The tragedies of Oedipus and Antigone explore topics of fate, free will, and the effects of human selections.

The heroes and heroines of Greek mythology span a huge spectrum of man or woman inclinations, from energy and valor to wit and cunning, from triumph to tragedy. Their testimonies maintain to resonate with us due to the fact they reflect the complexities and contradictions of human existence. As we journey through Greek mythology, we are able to encounter extra heroes and heroines, every with their non-public specific recollections and training to impart.

In the chapters that examine, we are able to delve further into the adventures, stressful conditions, and ethical dilemmas faced via those legendary figures. Their recollections offer us no longer only enjoyment however moreover insights into the human scenario, reminding us that heroism and tragedy are threads woven into the very fabric of our shared mythology.

Chapter 13: Greek Myths in Literature

The enduring enchantment of Greek mythology lies not most effective in its captivating tales but furthermore in its profound have an effect on on literature, paintings, and manner of lifestyles. From the earliest days of ancient Greece to the current international, Greek myths have served as a wellspring of concept, shaping the narratives and aesthetics of countless works of artwork and literature.

The Influence of Greek Mythology on Literature

Greek mythology's effect on literature is immeasurable, with its memories and archetypal characters offering a rich supply of cloth for authors across centuries and cultures. Here are a few incredible examples:

1. Homer's Epics: The epic poems "The Iliad" and "The Odyssey," attributed to the historic Greek poet Homer, are foundational texts of Western literature. They are steeped in Greek mythology, imparting heroes, gods, and the

epic struggles of the Trojan War. These poems set the volume for infinite next works of literature.

2. Greek Tragedies: Playwrights like Aeschylus, Sophocles, and Euripides crafted effective tragedies based on Greek myths. These works explored complicated subjects of destiny, morality, and the human situation. "Oedipus Rex" and "Antigone" via Sophocles, as an instance, delve into the tragic consequences of Oedipus's unknowing achievement of a prophecy.

three. Virgil's "Aeneid": While not Greek, the Roman poet Virgil's epic "Aeneid" draws intently from Greek mythology, blending it with Roman legends. The hero Aeneas's journey mirrors factors of Odysseus's adventures and consists of gods and characters from Greek delusion.

four. Shakespearean Influence: Even the works of William Shakespeare are endorsed with the resource of manner of Greek mythology. "A Midsummer Night's Dream" capabilities characters like Oberon and Titania, the king and queen of the fairies, drawn from classical mythology.

five. Modern Literature: Greek mythology keeps to inspire present day literature. Novels like Madeline Miller's "Circe" and "The Song of Achilles" re-agree with the lives of mythological figures, supplying sparkling perspectives on well-known testimonies.

Greek Myths in Ancient Greek Drama

Greek drama, in particular tragedies and comedies, often drew on Greek mythology for its trouble remember. These plays had been now not best a shape of entertainment however additionally a manner of exploring ethical and philosophical questions. The works of playwrights like Sophocles and Aristophanes live done and studied nowadays, imparting perception into the cultural importance of fable in ancient Greece.

Greek Mythological Motifs in Art and Sculpture

Greek mythology has left an indelible mark at the arena of visible arts. Ancient Greek sculptures, pottery, and frescoes often depicted mythological scenes and figures. Here are some super examples:

1. The Parthenon: The Parthenon, a temple committed to the goddess Athena, featured hard friezes that depicted scenes from Greek mythology, which incorporates the warfare a few of the Olympian gods and the Titans.

2. Pottery: Ancient Greek pottery often featured illustrations of mythological recollections, including the labors of Heracles, the adventures of Theseus, and scenes from the Trojan War.

3. Statuary: Classical Greek sculptures, consisting of the famous statue of Zeus at Olympia and the Venus de Milo, embodied the idealized human form and often represented mythological deities.

four. Renaissance Art: During the Renaissance, artists like Botticelli drew idea from Greek mythology. His painting "The Birth of Venus" depicts the goddess growing from the ocean on a shell, a scene immediately inspired by using way of historic mythology.

5. Neoclassicism: In the 18th and 19th centuries, the Neoclassical movement observed a revival of interest in Greek mythology. This have an effect on is obvious within the works of artists like Jacques-Louis David and John William Waterhouse.

Chapter 14: Lesser Deities and Creatures

While the Olympian gods and heroes frequently take middle degree in Greek mythology, the pantheon is teeming with a huge style of lesser deities and fantastical creatures. These beings inhabit the fringes of the mythic international, including intensity and range to the testimonies of ancient Greece. In this bankruptcy, we are able to find out a number of the ones lesser-identified but no plenty much less captivating figures.

The Muses: Inspirations of Art and Music

The Muses are a set of 9 goddesses who preside over the arts and sciences. Each Muse is related to a selected imaginitive venture, at the side of poetry, song, records, and dance. Artists and pupils may also invoke the Muses for idea and steering of their progressive endeavors. Their have an impact on on literature, track, and the highbrow hobbies of historical Greece is immeasurable.

The Fates and the Furies

The Fates, moreover called the Moirai, are 3 sisters—Clotho, Lachesis, and Atropos—who control the future of every mortal and immortal being. Clotho spins the thread of lifestyles, Lachesis measures it, and Atropos cuts it, symbolizing the inexorable march of destiny. They are impartial and unyielding, showing that even the gods are problem to destiny.

The Furies, or Erinyes, are avenging spirits who pursue those responsible of heinous crimes, mainly crimes inside the path of circle of relatives members. They are relentless in their pursuit of justice, regularly tormenting wrongdoers with madness and guilt till they face the results of their actions.

Nymphs and Satyrs

Nymphs are nature spirits who inhabit numerous natural features, which consist of forests, rivers, and mountains. There are precise varieties of nymphs, which include Naiads (water nymphs), Dryads (tree nymphs), and Nereids (sea nymphs). These ethereal beings are frequently associated with the splendor and energy of the natural world.

Satyrs, but, are 1/2-human, 1/2 of-animal creatures diagnosed for their love of revelry and mischief. They are frequently depicted as having the decrease frame of a goat and are partners of Dionysus, the god of wine and ecstasy. Satyrs are infamous for his or her irreverent conduct and are regularly featured in myths associated with wild and hedonistic celebrations.

Centaurs and Minotaurs

Centaurs are legendary creatures with the top frame of a human and the decrease body of a horse. They are identified for their energy and fight prowess. While a few centaurs, like Chiron, had been realistic and benevolent, others have been rowdy and susceptible to violence. Centaurs frequently appear in tales regarding Greek heroes and are symbolic of the twin nature of humanity.

The Minotaur, a widespread creature, is a part bull and detail human. It dwelled inside the labyrinth of King Minos at the island of Crete and changed into ultimately slain via Theseus. The Minotaur symbolizes the beastly and irrational factors of human nature and is a testament to the troubles of heroism and overcoming demanding situations found in Greek mythology.

The Chimera and Other Monsters

The Chimera is a fearsome hybrid monster with the frame of a lion, the pinnacle of a goat sprouting from its again, and a serpent's tail. It terrorized the location of Lycia till it modified into vanquished by way of the use of the hero Bellerophon with the aid of the winged horse Pegasus. The Chimera represents the chaos and unpredictability of the natural global.

Other extremely good monsters in Greek mythology consist of the Sphinx, a riddling creature who posed enigmatic questions to tourists; the Harpies, winged lady monsters who punished wrongdoers; and the Gorgons, 3 sisters with snakes for hair, the maximum well-known of whom emerge as Medusa.

The Sphinx and Riddles in Mythology

The Sphinx, a creature with the body of a lion, the wings of a bird, and the top of a woman, is renowned for her enigmatic riddles. She posed a riddle to all who approached her, and those who couldn't answer efficiently were devoured. It changed into the hero Oedipus who famously solved the Sphinx's riddle, incomes her wrath and in the end defeating her.

Riddles and puzzles often seem in Greek mythology as tests of wit and intelligence, reflecting the significance of cleverness and resourcefulness within the face of adversity.

Chapter 15: The Trojan War a Tale of Heroes and Destiny

The Trojan War is one of the most enduring and legendary conflicts in Greek mythology. Fought over the direction of ten years some of the metropolis of Troy and the Greek city-states, this epic conflict has captured the imaginations of storytellers, poets, and historians for millennia. In this financial catastrophe, we are capable of delve into the origins, events, and aftermath of the Trojan War, a tale that serves as a timeless testament to the interplay of future, heroism, and the capricious nature of the gods.

The Origins of the Trojan War

The seeds of the Trojan War had been sown in a story of splendor, competition, and divine discord. The root purpose of the conflict changed into the kidnapping of Helen, the maximum lovely girl within the global, with the useful resource of using Paris, a prince of Troy. Helen, however, has become already married to Menelaus, the king of Sparta, and her abduction delivered approximately a vow of revenge.

The Judgment of Paris is a pivotal 2nd inside the lead-as a good deal as the war. Paris have grow to be requested to choose which of three goddesses—Aphrodite, Hera, and Athena—have emerge as the most lovely. He determined on Aphrodite, who promised him the love of the most lovely mortal girl, Helen. This desire set in motion the collection of activities that would culminate inside the Trojan War.

The Greek Expedition to Troy

In reaction to the abduction of Helen and the mild to Menelaus, the Greek metropolis-states lengthy-installed a coalition led thru King Agamemnon of Mycenae. This alliance, which covered heroes collectively with Achilles, Odysseus, Ajax, and Diomedes, set sail for Troy to retrieve Helen and precise vengeance.

The Greeks faced severa demanding situations and boundaries inside the direction in their journey to Troy, which includes storms, monsters, and divine interventions. The journey itself is a testament to the onerous nature of heroic quests in Greek mythology.

The War Rages On

Once the Greek forces arrived at Troy, the battle raged on for ten prolonged years. The war grow to be marked via the use of using epic battles, heroic deeds, and the intervention of the gods. Notable sports activities at some point of the struggle covered:

The duel among Paris and Menelaus, which grow to be interrupted by the usage of the goddess Aphrodite, who whisked Paris far from the battlefield.

The rage of Achilles, one of the nice Greek warriors, who withdrew from the stopping in protest of Agamemnon's moves. Achilles' absence had a profound effect on the course of the conflict.

The heroics of Hector, the Trojan prince and defender of Troy, who confronted Achilles in a tragic showdown.

The cunning of Odysseus, who devised the concept of the Trojan Horse, a massive wooden horse concealing Greek soldiers internal. The Trojans unwittingly introduced the pony inside their town walls, most important to Troy's downfall.

The Fall of Troy

The fall of Troy marked the give up result of the battle. After ten years of conflict, the Greeks devised a stratagem to infiltrate the metropolis. The Greeks hid themselves inside the Trojan Horse, which modified into left as an offering to the gods out of doors the town gates. The Trojans, believing the war became over and that the pony changed into a picture of victory, added it into the metropolis.

That night, due to the fact the Trojans celebrated, the Greek infantrymen emerged from the pony and opened the gates for the Greek navy, which had decrease returned below the duvet of darkness. The town of Troy modified into sacked, and a lot of its inhabitants were killed or enslaved. The destiny of Troy served as a reminder of the capriciousness of destiny and the consequences of human movements.

The Heroes and Their Fates

The heroes of the Trojan War have been no longer exempt from the inexorable forces of destiny. Achilles, who had the choice of either an extended, unremarkable life or a short but exquisite one, decided on the latter. His loss of existence in battle emerge as foretold, and it got here to bypass while Paris, guided with the resource of way of Apollo, shot him with an arrow in the willing heel.

Hector, too, faced a unhappy prevent at the hands of Achilles, irrespective of his valor and devotion to his own family and town. The battle's very last outcomes, stimulated through manner of divine machinations and human choices, illustrated the complicated interplay amongst future and free will.

The Aftermath and Legacy of the Trojan War

The give up of the Trojan War marked a cross lower back to the Greek heroes' homes, but their journeys had been a long way from over. Odysseus's ten-one year voyage domestic to Ithaca, chronicled in Homer's "Odyssey," is one of the maximum enduring and epic memories of this era.

The Trojan War left an extended-lasting legacy in Greek lifestyle and literature. It served as a backdrop for the superb works of Homer, and its difficulty topics of heroism, destiny, and the effects of war persevered to resonate in next generations. The conflict additionally left an indelible mark at the area of artwork and drama, with limitless performs, poems, and works of artwork inspired through its epic narratives.

The Trojan War is a saga of heroes and heroines, gods and mortals, destiny and tragedy. It embodies the complexities and contradictions of the human revel in, in which the pursuit of honor and vengeance can result in unimaginable outcomes. The warfare's legacy endures as a timeless and cautionary story, a testament to the iconic energy of delusion to find out the profound questions that define our existence.

As we reflect on the Trojan War, we preserve to discover the layers of its tale, its characters, and its training. Join me as we find out further into the location of Greek mythology, in which the echoes of this epic struggle reverberate through the long time, and wherein the heroic spirit lives on.

Chapter 16: Love and Desire

Greek mythology is replete with reminiscences of affection and preference, each divine and mortal. The gods and goddesses themselves were no longer proof against the passions that gripped the hearts of mortals, and their romantic entanglements often brought on dramatic and occasionally tragic consequences. In this bankruptcy, we find out the subject subjects of love, desire, and the complexities of relationships inside the global of Greek mythology.

Aphrodite, the Goddess of Love

Aphrodite, the goddess of love and beauty, held a main characteristic in Greek mythology's romantic narratives. She have become born from the ocean foam near the island of Cyprus and modified into the epitome of physical and emotional appeal. Aphrodite's splendor becomes remarkable, and she or he or he possessed the electricity to stir preference and passion in every gods and mortals.

Her romantic pastimes spanned the divine and mortal geographical regions. She comes to be married to Hephaestus, the god of fireplace and smiting, but her heart belonged to Ares, the god of battle. Aphrodite's passionate affair with Ares turns out to be a supply of scandal maximum of the gods and frequently ended in tumultuous activities.

Eros and Psyche: Love beyond Mortality

The tale of Eros, the god of affection, and Psyche, a mortal princess, is a tale of love that transcended the limits of mortality. Eros fell in love with Psyche, but their dating turn out to be to start with saved mystery. Psyche's hobby approximately her unseen lover brought about a sequence of trials, together with a descent into the underworld.

Their tale in the long run culminated in Psyche's transformation into an immortal, and he or she or he and Eros had been united in eternal love. The delusion of Eros and Psyche explores topics of take into account, interest, and the transformative energy of affection.

Orpheus and Eurydice: Love's Tragic Quest

Orpheus, a legendary musician and poet, have become recognized for his outstanding know-how. His love for Eurydice, a mortal female, modified into deep and passionate Tragically, Eurydice died from snakebite shortly after their bridal ceremony. Overcome with grief, Orpheus journeyed to the underworld to plead with Hades and Persephone for her move back.

Hades agreed to allow Eurydice go on one situation: Orpheus have to lead her out of the underworld without searching decrease again till they reached the area of the residing. In a 2nd of doubt and tension, Orpheus glanced once more, causing Eurydice to be out of place to him all the time. Their story is a poignant reminder of the fragility of love and the outcomes of doubt and hesitation.

Pyramus and Thisbe: Forbidden Love

The tragic tale of Pyramus and Thisbe is a story of forbidden love and miscommunication These more youthful fanatics, who lived in neighboring homes within the city of Babylon, have been deeply in love but were stored apart via way of their feuding households. They communicated through a crack in the wall that separated their homes.

Their ill-fated try and meet each different in mystery, below a mulberry tree, led to a heartbreaking false impression. Thisbe arrived first and come to be worried through a lioness, leaving in the back of her veil. When Pyramus arrived and observed the bloody veil, he believed Thisbe to be useless and took his very non-public life. Thisbe, returning to discover her cherished useless, moreover decided on to surrender her existence. Their tragic deaths united their families in grief and taken about the change they'd favored in life.

Narcissus and Echo: The Pitfalls of Self-Love

The tale of Narcissus, a greater younger guy acknowledged for his terrific splendor, is a cautionary tale about the risks of excessive self-love. Narcissus modified into so enamored together with his very private mirrored image that he couldn't tear himself away from it. Eventually, he wasted away and died, pining for the improbable photograph he noticed inside the water.

Echo, a nymph who has been cursed via the use of the use of Hera to only repeat the phrases of others, fell in love with Narcissus but need to first-rate echo his phrases lower back to him. Her unrequited love and Narcissus's self-obsession delivered approximately their tragic fates. The time period "narcissism" is derived from this fable and is used to give an explanation for excessive self-love and vanity.

Love and choice are vital components of the human experience, and Greek mythology explores those troubles thru a diverse array of characters and narratives. From the passions of the gods to the tragedies of mortal fans, these memories mirror the complexities of human relationships, the strength of love to transform and transcend, and the consequences of obsession and miscommunication.

As we journey deeper into the area of Greek mythology, we are able to keep to come across testimonies of love and preference, each presenting its personal precise insights into the human coronary heart and the everlasting quest for connection and success.

Chapter 17: The Quests and Adventures

Greek mythology is replete with quests and adventures that test the mettle of heroes and heroines, difficult them to overcome ambitious obstacles and show their worthiness. These quests take them to remote lands, into the heart of chance, and regularly into the arena of the divine. In this monetary catastrophe, we delve into a number of the most legendary quests and adventures in Greek mythology.

The Quest for the Golden Fleece

The quest for the Golden Fleece is one of the maximum famous and enduring recollections of heroism in Greek mythology. Jason, the rightful heir to the throne of Iolchus, released into this epic journey to retrieve the Golden Fleece, a symbol of kingship.

To accomplish this project, Jason assembled a team of heroes referred to as the Argonauts and sailed aboard the supply Argo. Their quest led them to the remote land of Colchis, wherein the fleece modified into guarded through a dragon. With the help of the sorceress Medea, Jason successfully retrieved the fleece, overcoming severa trials and adversaries.

The quest for the Golden Fleece symbolizes the hero's adventure to advantage a noble purpose, the assistance of supernatural allies, and the eventual success of destiny.

The Twelve Labors of Heracles (Hercules)

Heracles, referred to as Hercules in Roman mythology, is possibly the most celebrated of all Greek heroes. His legendary power and endurance had been each a blessing and a curse, as he end up driven to carry out twelve labors as punishment for a healthful of madness resulting from the goddess Hera.

These labors were a sequence of amazing responsibilities, in conjunction with slaying the Nemean Lion, taking pictures the Erymanthian Boar, and cleaning the Augean Stables, among others. Each labor showcased Heracles' indomitable spirit, valor, and resourcefulness. His adventure turned into definitely one of redemption and atonement, as he sought to show his worthiness and triumph over his flaws.

The Adventures of Perseus

Perseus, the son of Zeus and Danaë, released into a sequence of exceptional adventures that showcased his foxy and heroism. His most well-known quest become to slay the Gorgon Medusa, a massive creature with snakes for hair whose gaze have become humans to stone.

With the useful beneficial aid of divine items, along with a reflective guard, winged sandals, and a mystical sword, Perseus ventured into the perilous lair of Medusa. He ultimately triumphed over her, the usage of her severed head as a weapon. Perseus's adventures also protected rescuing the princess Andromeda from a sea monster and encountering severa different demanding situations.

The Labors of Theseus: Slayer of the Minotaur

Theseus, regarded for his wit and bravery, is excellent stated for his quest to slay the Minotaur, a massive creature with the frame of a person and the pinnacle of a bull. The Minotaur turn out to be imprisoned within the labyrinthine palace of King Minos in Crete.

Guided via the usage of the love of Princess Ariadne and armed with a sword and a ball of thread, Theseus correctly navigated the labyrinth and slew the Minotaur, making sure the protection of his fellow Athenians. This heroic feat exemplifies the triumph of courage and foxy over insurmountable odds, in addition to the hero's obligation to protect and shop his humans.

The Odyssey: Odysseus' Homeward Journey

Following the sports of the Trojan War, the hero Odysseus launched into a protracted and tough adventure domestic to his liked spouse, Penelope, and his u . S . A . Of Ithaca. His ten-365 days odyssey, chronicled in Homer's "Odyssey," is a testament to wit, foxy, and perseverance.

Odysseus confronted severa trials and obstacles, which includes encounters with legendary creatures just like the Cyclops Polyphemus, the sorceress Circe, and the sirens who lured sailors to their doom. His very last return domestic have grow to be a triumph of intelligence and resourcefulness, exemplifying the hero's quest to conquer adversity and reunite together collectively together with his circle of relatives.

The quests and adventures of Greek mythology shipping us to a worldwide of heroic deeds, perilous trips, and epic traumatic conditions. These reminiscences encourage us with tales of valor, cunning, and the indomitable human spirit. Whether it's the pursuit of a golden fleece, the of entirety of herculean labors, or the voyage domestic from a decade-lengthy struggle, those quests are emblematic of the hero's path and the human choice to conquer the unknown.

www.ingramcontent.com/pod-product-compliance
Lightning Source LLC
Chambersburg PA
CBHW071442080526
44587CB00014B/1948